SINGER

SEWING REFERENCE LIBRARY®

The New Sewing *with a* Serger

CREATIVE PUBLISHING international

CHANHASSEN, MINNESOTA

www.creativepub.com

SINGER

SEWING REFERENCE LIBRARY®

The New Sewing *with a* Serger

Contents

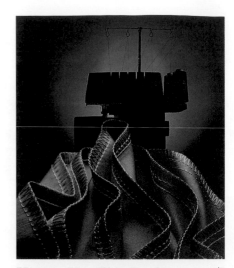

President/CEO: Michael Eleftheriou
Vice President/Publisher: Linda Ball
Vice President/Retail Sales: Kevin Haas

Copyright © 1998
Creative Publishing international, Inc.
18705 Lake Drive East
Chanhassen, Minnesota 55317
1-800-328-3895
www.creativepub.com
All rights reserved
Printed in U.S.A.

Library of Congress Cataloging-in-Publication Data
The new sewing with a serger.
      p. cm. -- (Singer sewing reference library)
      Rev. ed. of: Sewing with an overlock. 1989.
      Includes index.
      ISBN 0-86573-329-5 (hardcover) – ISBN 0-86573-330-9 (pbk. : alk. paper)
      1. Serging. I. Sewing with an overlock. II. Creative Publishing
International. III. Title: Sewing with a serger. IV. Series.
TT713.N47 1998
646.2'044--dc21   98-40898

Books available in this series:
  Sewing Essentials, Sewing for the Home, Clothing Care & Repair, Sewing for Style, Sewing Specialty Fabrics, Sewing Activewear, The Perfect Fit, Timesaving Sewing, More Sewing for the Home, Tailoring, Sewing for Children, 101 Sewing Secrets, Sewing Pants That Fit, Quilting by Machine, Decorative Machine Stitching, Creative Sewing Ideas, Sewing Lingerie, Sewing Projects for the Home, Sewing with Knits, More Creative Sewing Ideas, Quilt Projects by Machine, Creating Fashion Accessories, Quick & Easy Sewing Projects, Sewing for Special Occasions, Sewing for the Holidays, Quick & Easy Decorating Projects, Quilted Projects & Garments, Embellished Quilted Projects, Window Treatments, Holiday Projects, Halloween Costumes, Upholstery Basics, Fabric Artistry, The New Sewing with a Serger

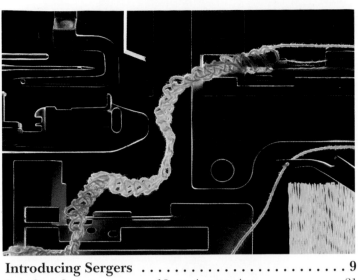

THE NEW SEWING WITH A SERGER

Created by: The Editors of Creative Publishing international, Inc., in cooperation with the Sewing Education Department, Singer Sewing Company. Singer is a trademark of The Singer Company Limited and is used under license.

Executive Editor: Elaine Perry
Senior Editor: Linda Neubauer
Project Manager: Jill Anderson
Senior Art Director: Delores Swanson
Editor/Writer: Nancy Sundeen
Copy Editor: Janice Cauley
Lead Project & Prop Stylist: Joanne Wawra
Project & Prop Stylist: Christine Jahns
Sample Production Manager: Elizabeth Reichow
Lead Samplemaker: Phyllis Galbraith

Samplemakers: Arlene Dohrman, Sharon Eklund, Bridget Haugh, Virginia Mateen, Delores Minkema
Senior Technical Photo Stylist: Bridget Haugh
Technical Photo Stylists: Sharon Eklund, Nancy Sundeen
Studio Services Manager: Marcia Chambers
Photo Services Coordinator: Carol Osterhus
Photographers: Tate Carlson, Rex Irmen, Andrea Rugg, Greg Wallace
Manager, Production Services: Kim Gerber
Production Staff: Curt Ellering, Laura Hokkanen, Kay Wethern
Desktop Publishing Specialist: Laurie Kristensen
Consultant: Becky Hanson
Contributors: Burda Patterns; Chandlers Shoes; Clotilde; Coats & Clark; DMC Corporation;

Environmental Lighting Concepts, Inc.; Gingher, Inc.; Kwik Sew Pattern Company; Madeira; The McCall Pattern Company; Minnetonka Mills, Inc.; Pentapco, Inc.; Rowenta, Inc.; Simplicity Pattern Company, Inc.; The Singer Sewing Company; Swiss-Metrosene, Inc.; Tacony Corporation; Vogue/Butterick Patterns; William E. Wright Co.; YLI Corporation

Printed on American paper by:
R. R. Donnelley
10 9 8

How to Use This Book

Sergers appeared on the home-sewing market in the 1970s. Since then, many different types of machines have been introduced, including machines that use three, four, and five threads. Differential feed is now available on most models, and a variety of specialized presser feet make sewing tasks easy.

Look through *The New Sewing with a Serger* for inspiration and ideas. The step-by-step photographs will help you learn up-to-date methods for serging and how to identify stitch problems. Contrasting thread has been used in many of the photos so the stitches can be seen easily.

Introducing Sergers

The first section of this book, Introducing Sergers, shows you the kinds of sewing that can be done on a serger. You can stitch seams, trim seam allowances, and finish seams all in one step. Learn how a serger works, and discover the variety of stitches it can make, from standard seams to professional hems.

If you already own a serger, you may discover new ways to use it. Or, if you are considering buying one, this section may help you decide whether serger sewing is for you. It offers helpful tips for buying a serger, using the accessories, selecting just the right thread, and caring for your machine.

You will be introduced to a new vocabulary and even learn how to arrange your sewing room to accommodate the extra machine.

Basic Serger Techniques

At first, you may be intimidated by this new piece of equipment. The section, Basic Serger Techniques, helps you through the getting-acquainted process. You can easily learn the quick threading and rethreading techniques and avoid the common threading mistakes that cause stitching problems.

There are special techniques developed for trimming away just the right amount of fabric, for sewing seams,

hems, corners, and curves, even for removing stitches the easy way. Practice these methods before sewing a garment to gain confidence and skill.

Adjusting the Stitches

To achieve the best results on each fabric, adjust the stitch length, width, and tension according to the guidelines in the section, Adjusting the Stitches. These pages can serve as a reference as you continue to work with new fabrics and stitches.

This section will help you develop confidence in adjusting the tension dials. Learn what the correct tension looks like for each stitch type and how to adjust your machine to achieve good stitches.

Garment Construction

A serger makes sewing more efficient than ever before. Discover new methods for stitching collars, hems, cuffs, plackets, waistbands, and waistlines. The section, Garment Construction, includes step-by-step instructions for using your serger to make pullover tops, blouses, skirts, dresses, and activewear.

Find out how to serge special fabrics, such as silkies, sheers, swimwear, and laces. Learn how easy it is to sew sweaters using the sweater knit fabrics and sweater bodies that sergers handle so beautifully.

Special Effects

Enjoy creating one-of-a-kind garments with the special effects of decorative stitching. Learn how to achieve custom finishes with your serger using special threads, such as texturized nylon, rayon, silk, metallic, and topstitching thread, and even ribbon and yarn.

Use the troubleshooting chart when you encounter a stitch problem. With this quick checklist, most problems can be easily solved.

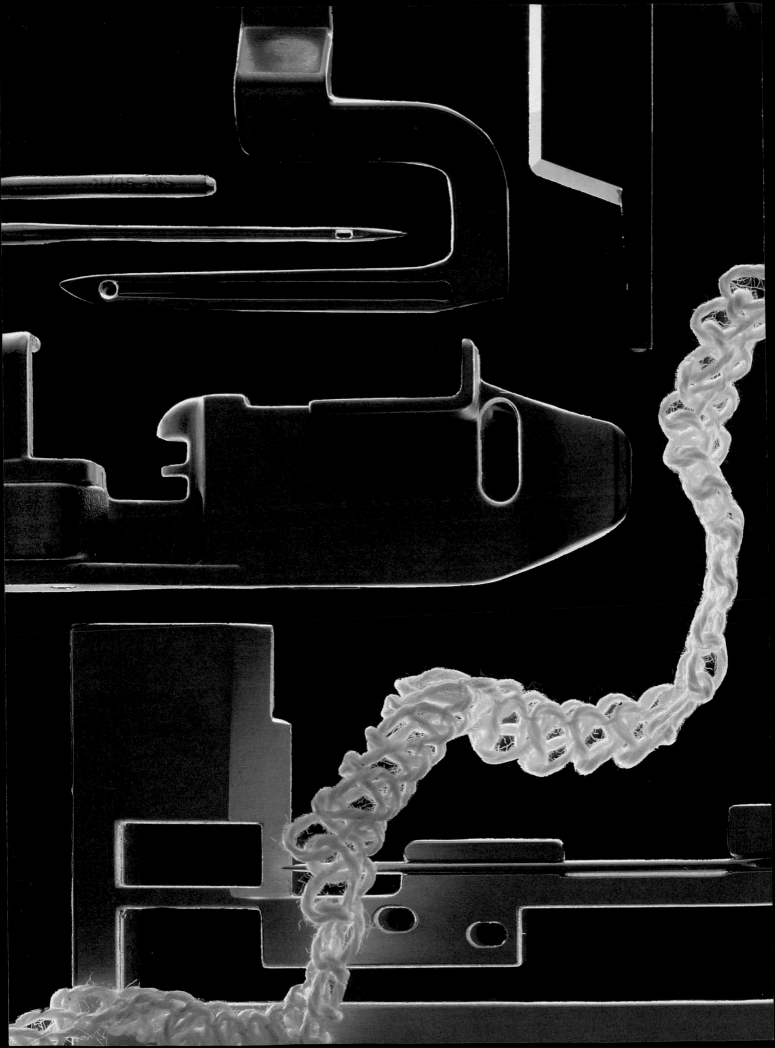

Introducing Sergers

Uses for a Serger

Many busy home sewers want to save time when sewing but are not willing to sacrifice quality. Sergers, sometimes called overlock machines, offer the special stitches of ready-to-wear with faster and easier construction methods.

These machines can sew seams at 1500 stitches per minute, trimming and overcasting the raw edges at the same time for quality seam finishes. Used side by side with your conventional sewing machine, a serger can add new excitement to home sewing.

Fabrics you previously avoided can be sewn quickly and easily. Sergers are excellent for stitching seams with built-in stretch for T-shirts and swimwear made from knit fabric. They also excel at sewing all types of woven fabrics, from sheers and silkies to heavy denims.

In addition to the basic stitches for seams and seam finishes, alternative hem stitches and decorative flatlock stitches are also available to add special details to your sewing projects.

Overedge seam finishes add the look of ready-to-wear to unlined garments.

Pucker-free seams on silky fabrics are fast and easy to sew on a serger.

Flatlock stitching with decorative thread is used for a special effect.

Rolled hems are narrow, neat edge finishes for ruffles and hems.

Sweater knit fabrics and ribbings are sewn without fear of the fabric raveling.

Serged seams are stitched as selvages are trimmed away. Differential feed makes gathers easy.

Overlock stitches that stretch are perfect for sewing swim-wear from two-way stretch knit fabric.

The Serger

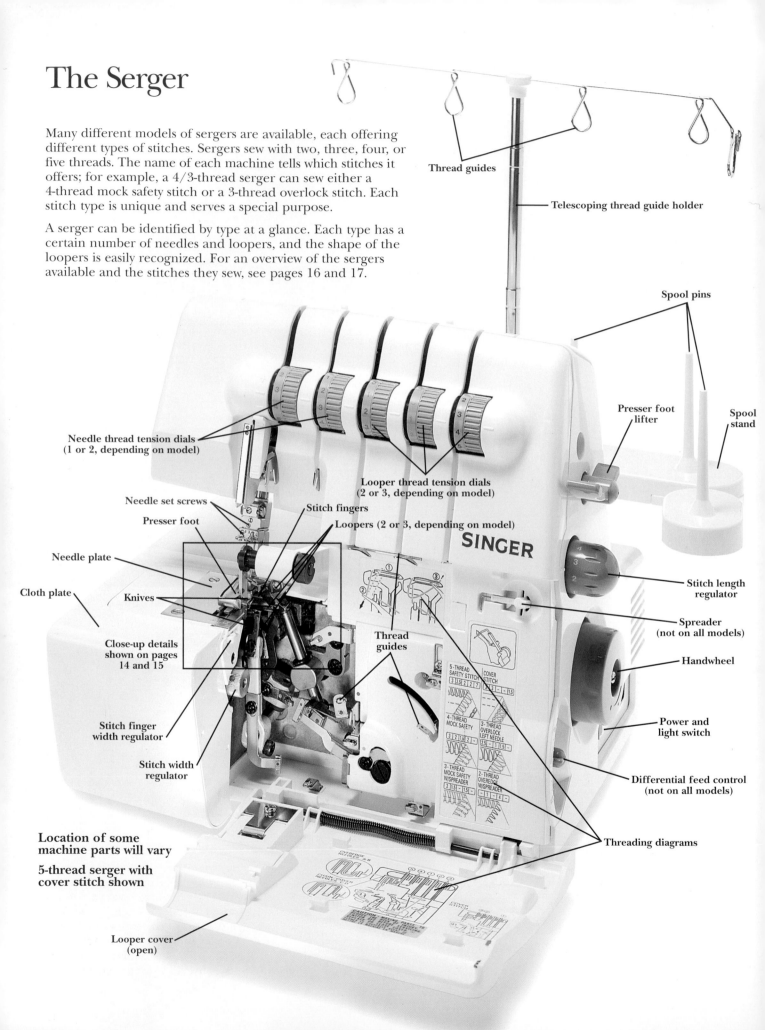

Many different models of sergers are available, each offering different types of stitches. Sergers sew with two, three, four, or five threads. The name of each machine tells which stitches it offers; for example, a 4/3-thread serger can sew either a 4-thread mock safety stitch or a 3-thread overlock stitch. Each stitch type is unique and serves a special purpose.

A serger can be identified by type at a glance. Each type has a certain number of needles and loopers, and the shape of the loopers is easily recognized. For an overview of the sergers available and the stitches they sew, see pages 16 and 17.

Thread guides

Telescoping thread guide holder

Spool pins

Presser foot lifter

Spool stand

Needle thread tension dials (1 or 2, depending on model)

Looper thread tension dials (2 or 3, depending on model)

Needle set screws

Stitch fingers

Presser foot

Loopers (2 or 3, depending on model)

Needle plate

Cloth plate

Knives

Close-up details shown on pages 14 and 15

Stitch length regulator

Spreader (not on all models)

Handwheel

Thread guides

Power and light switch

Stitch finger width regulator

Stitch width regulator

Differential feed control (not on all models)

Threading diagrams

Location of some machine parts will vary

5-thread serger with cover stitch shown

Looper cover (open)

How to Identify Types of Sergers

3-thread serger has one needle and two loopers: an upper looper (**a**) and a lower looper (**b**). It sews a 3-thread overlock stitch; some models, called 3/2-thread sergers, convert to sew the 2-thread overedge stitch.

4/3-thread serger has two needles and two loopers: an upper looper (**a**) and a lower looper (**b**). It sews a 4-thread mock safety stitch similar to the 3-thread overlock stitch; an extra needle thread secures the stitches. It sews the 3-thread overlock stitch when only one needle is used. A 4/3/2-thread serger also sews the 2-thread overedge stitch.

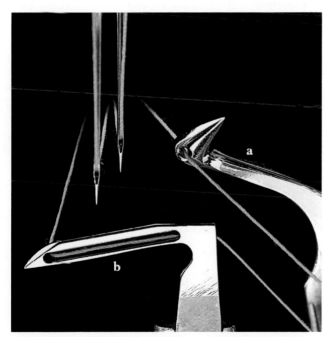

4/2-thread serger has two needles and two loopers: an upper looper (**a**) and a chainstitch lower looper (**b**). It sews a 4-thread safety stitch consisting of a 2-thread chainstitch and a 2-thread overedge, which are stitched simultaneously. The chainstitch and the overedge stitch can each be used separately. This serger will not sew a 3-thread overlock stitch.

5-thread serger has two needles and three loopers: an upper looper (**a**); a lower looper (**b**); and a chainstitch looper (**c**). It sews a 5-thread safety stitch with a 2-thread chainstitch and a 3-thread overlock stitch. Some 5-thread machines also sew a 4-thread safety stitch, a 2-thread overedge stitch, and a 4-thread or 3-thread mock safety stitch. Each stitch may be used separately. Some 5-thread sergers convert to sew the cover stitch.

Feed system. Feed dogs, needle plate, and presser foot work together to move fabric with even feeding.

Some machines have a differential feed system to prevent puckered or stretched seams.

How Sergers Work

Sergers perform many functions simultaneously to create stitches. As the fabric is fed into the machine, it reaches the feed dogs first. The fabric is moved along until the knives trim the edge. Then the loopers and needles form the stitches on the fabric, and the fabric is fed off the stitch fingers behind the needle.

Cutting system. Seam allowances are trimmed with movable upper knife (**a**) and stationary lower knife (**b**); knives work together, like scissors, at the same speed as the needle moves.

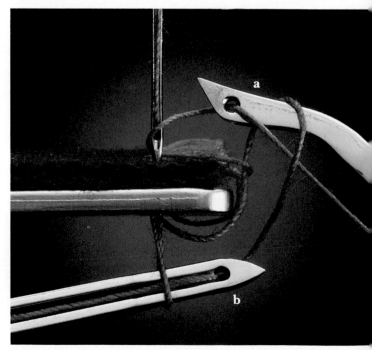

Loopers. Upper looper (**a**) and lower looper (**b**) are used instead of a bobbin to form the stitches. Looper and needle threads lock together to sew seams or seam finishes. Looper threads do not penetrate the fabric.

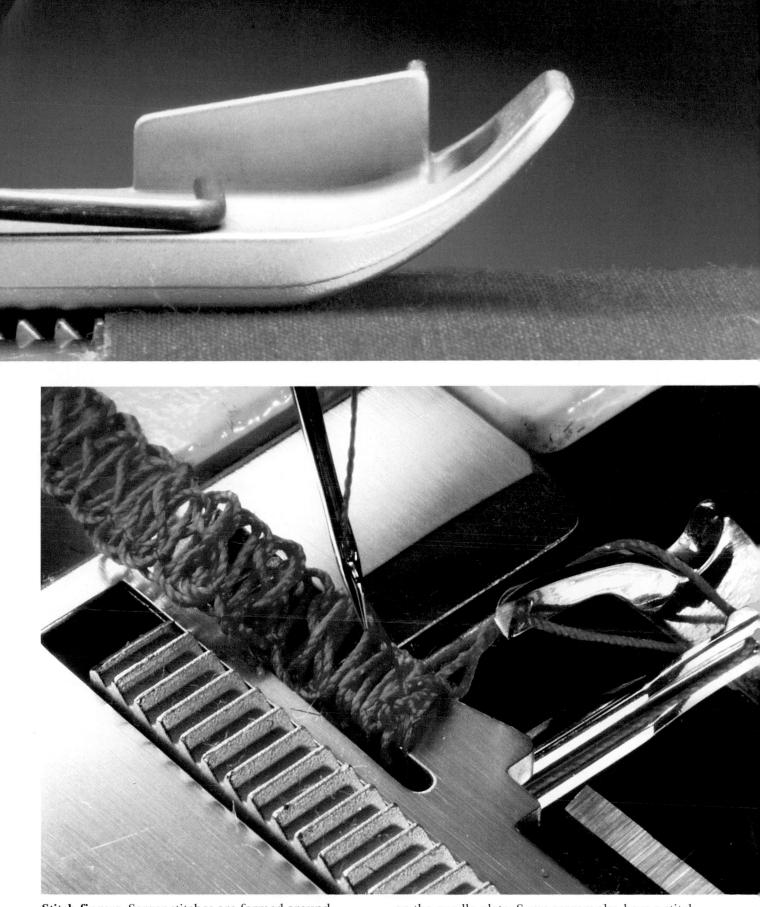

Stitch fingers. Serger stitches are formed around one or two stitch fingers, small projections or prongs on the needle plate. Some sergers also have a stitch finger on the presser foot.

The Stitches & Their Uses

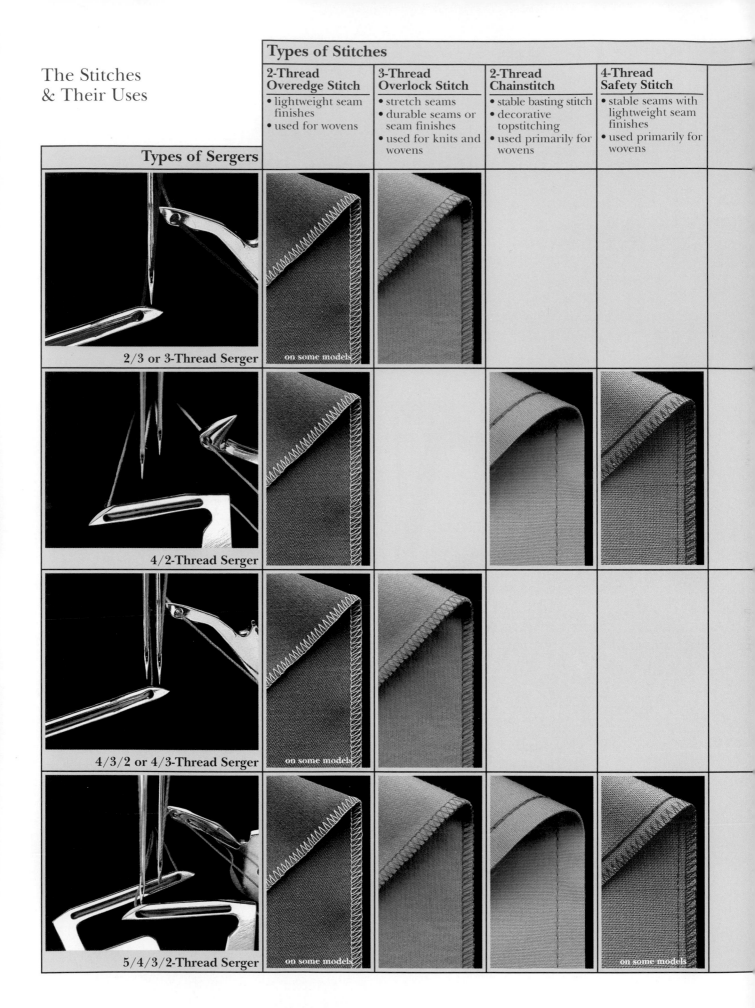

Types of Sergers	Types of Stitches			
	2-Thread Overedge Stitch • lightweight seam finishes • used for wovens	**3-Thread Overlock Stitch** • stretch seams • durable seams or seam finishes • used for knits and wovens	**2-Thread Chainstitch** • stable basting stitch • decorative topstitching • used primarily for wovens	**4-Thread Safety Stitch** • stable seams with lightweight seam finishes • used primarily for wovens
2/3 or 3-Thread Serger	on some models			
4/2-Thread Serger	on some models			
4/3/2 or 4/3-Thread Serger	on some models			
5/4/3/2-Thread Serger	on some models			on some models

5-Thread Safety Stitch	3-Thread Mock Safety Stitch	4-Thread Mock Safety Stitch	Flatlock Stitch	Rolled Hem Stitch	Cover Stitch
• stable seams with durable seam finishes • used primarily for wovens	• durable ultra-stretch seams • used for super-stretch knits like Lycra® or spandex	• durable stretch seams • used for knits and wovens	• flat, nonbulky stretch seams • decorative stitching • used primarily for knits	• narrow hems and seams • decorative stitching • used for knits and wovens	• stretch hems and seams • decorative stitching, trims • used primarily for knits
	 on some models				
		 on some models			 on some models

| 5-Thread Safety Stitch | 3-Thread Mock Safety Stitch | 4-Thread Mock Safety Stitch | | Flatlock Stitch | Rolled Hem Stitch | Cover Stitch |

Buying a Serger

When shopping for a serger, keep in mind the same basic questions you would ask if buying a conventional sewing machine. Shop with an assortment of woven and knit fabric scraps of various weights. Tell the dealer what type of sewing you plan to do and which fabrics you usually use. Test several models and note how the machines handle the fabrics.

Sergers appear very different from conventional machines, and you may feel more comfortable if someone is willing to guide you through the learning process. Learn how to thread the machine from start to finish, and turn the tension dials at random to see how easily you can restore the perfect stitch. Ask the dealer to explain the stitch width and length controls, because they do vary from model to model.

Various special features are available on sergers. Have all features, such as differential feed, rolled hem, and cover stitch, explained and demonstrated; learn what adjustments are required for changing from one to another. Compare features from model to model to be sure that the machine you purchase will meet your needs.

Some features may be more important to you than others, depending on the type of sewing you want to do. For example, differential feed, available on many models, speeds your sewing if you frequently gather fabric, and it is helpful for preventing puckered seams on silky fabrics or stretched seams on sweater knits.

You will find it easier to ask pertinent questions and to understand the dealer demonstrations if you are familiar with how sergers work. Read about the different types of machines and the stitches they sew (pages 12 to 17) before you shop. Also check the chart, below, to become familiar with the vocabulary used to define the parts of the machine and its various stitches.

Your satisfaction with your serger will depend, to a great extent, on your dealer. It is important to purchase a serger from a dealer you like and trust, since you are also buying the service and experience of that dealer. Find out if lessons are available; ask questions during the lessons to be sure everything is clear. Find out who does the repair service.

The Vocabulary

Balanced stitch. A stitch that is adjusted so threads lock together at the edge of the fabric.

Bite. Another name for stitch width.

Chainstitch. A stitch sewn on a 4/2-thread or 5-thread machine that interlocks the left needle thread with the chain looper thread. This stitch does not overlock the fabric edge.

Converter. Another name for a spreader.

Cover stitch. A specialty stitch that does not trim or overedge; the upper knife is disengaged and two needle threads create parallel rows of stitching secured by a lower looper thread.

Differential feed. A feature available on many models that prevents puckered or stretched seams and is used to gather fabrics.

Flatlock stitch. A special decorative stitch that allows the fabric to be pulled flat. It shows a looped thread on one side of the fabric and ladder stitches on the other side.

Knives. The two blades of a serger that trim or cut the fabric just before the stitches are formed.

Ladder stitches. The short parallel stitch formation seen on the underside of a flatlock stitch.

Loopers. Parts of a serger that deliver threads to interlock with needle threads. Loopers do not pierce the fabric; the upper looper thread sits on the top side of the fabric and the lower looper thread sits on the underside.

Mock safety stitch. Commonly, the 4-thread ultra-stretch stitch sewn on a 4/3/2-thread serger; a 3-thread mock safety stitch is also available on some models. The 3-thread stitch will stretch farther than the 4-thread stitch.

Overcast stitch. Another name for overedge stitch.

Overedge stitch. A stitch that finishes the edge of the fabric to prevent raveling but is not used for seaming.

Overlock machine. Another name for a serger.

Overlock stitch. A stitch that locks together at the edge of the seam allowance, finishing the edges as well as sewing the seam.

Rolled hem stitch. A stitch that rolls under the edge of the fabric and covers it with thread.

Safety stitch. Another name for chainstitch.

Serger. A sewing machine that simultaneously stitches, trims, and finishes seams.

Spreader. A feature of some serger models that blocks the eye of the upper looper during the formation of reduced-thread stitches. The lower looper thread is forced to serve as the upper looper thread; two-thread versions of stitches that usually require three or four threads reduce bulk and improve stretchability.

Stitch finger. The metal prong or prongs on the needle plate or presser foot. Stitches form around the stitch finger and the fabric edge at the same time. Completed stitch is fed off the back of the finger.

Stitch length. The distance in millimeters between needle penetrations.

Stitch width. The distance in millimeters between needle thread and the trimmed edge of the fabric.

Tail chain. Stitches, formed over the stitch finger, that are locked together and left on the machine after the seam is completed.

Tension dial. The part of the machine that is turned to adjust the tension of each thread.

Tension disc. An internal pressure plate in the tension assembly. Each disc is adjusted by turning the tension dial, creating pressure, or tension, on the thread to regulate stitch formation.

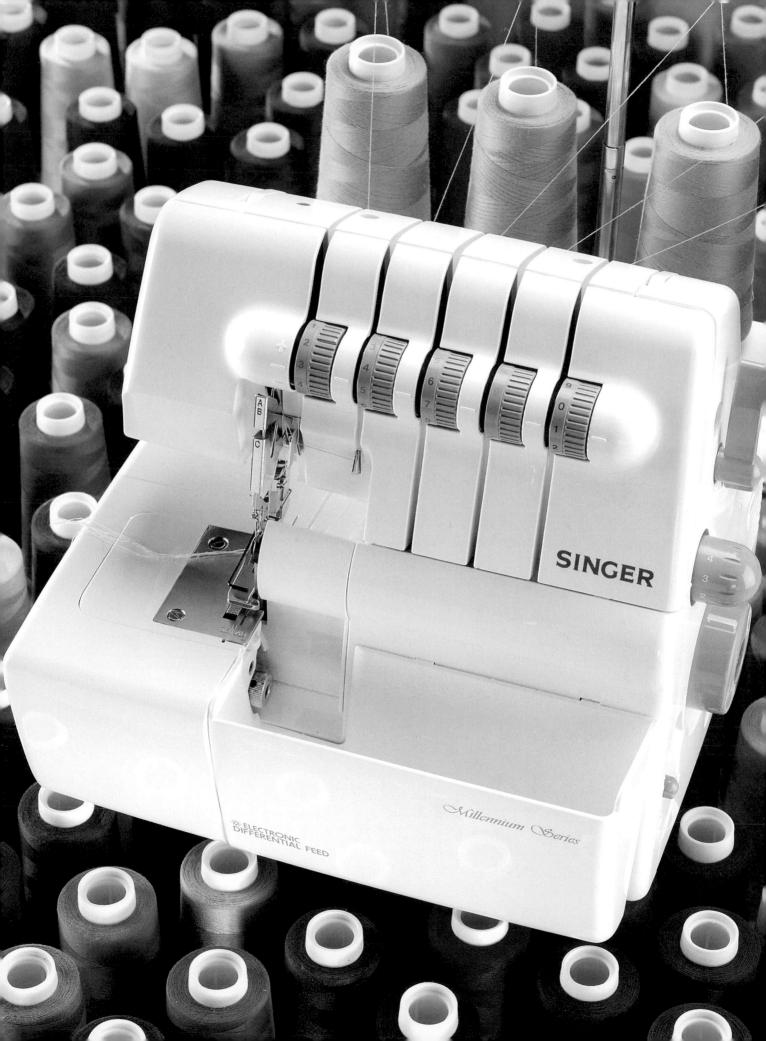

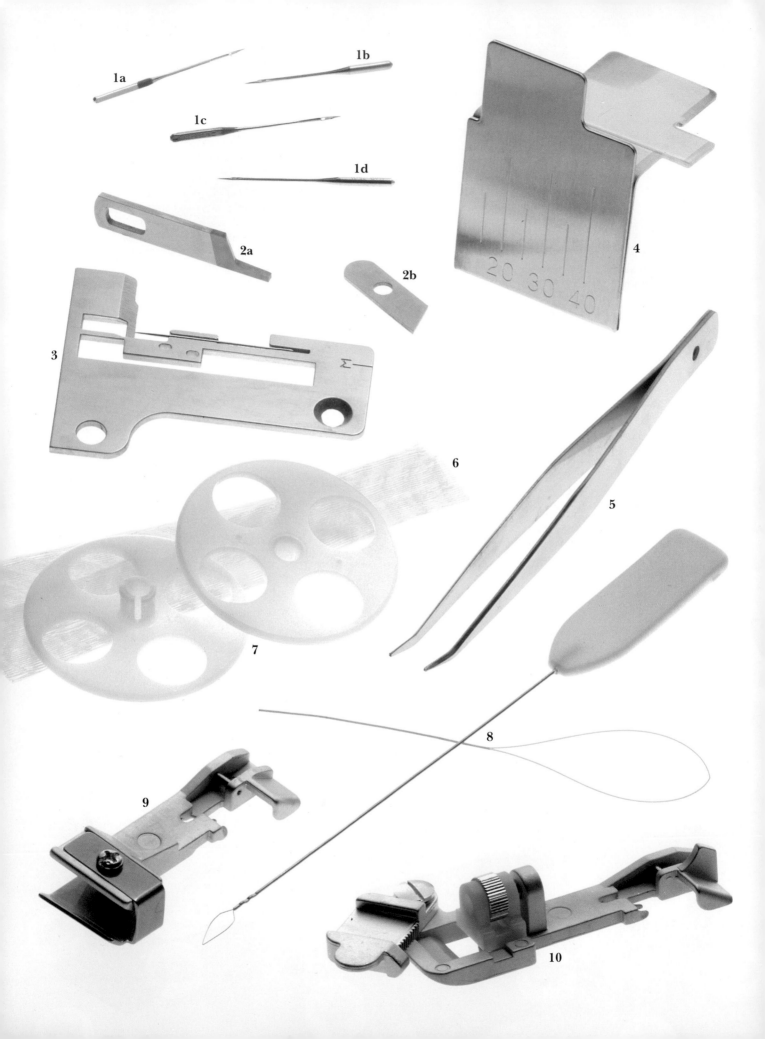

Accessories

Every serger comes with an accessory kit. The instruction manual that comes with the machine describes the use for each tool. The accessories supplied with a serger will vary, depending on the model. Learning to use them correctly will make sewing time more productive.

Needles vary from one model to another. Industrial needles are available with flat **(1a)** or round **(1b)** shank. Conventional sewing machine needles **(1c)** and special embroidery needles with a long eye **(1d)** can be used in some sergers. Check the serger instruction manual for the correct type of needle to be used in your machine.

Knives trim the excess seam allowances before the seam is stitched. The upper blade **(2a)** is movable and cuts against the stationary lower blade **(2b)** with the same action as scissors.

Rolled hem plate (3) is necessary when the rolled hem stitch is not a built-in feature. Some brands may also require the use of a rolled hem presser foot. These attachments may or may not come with the machine at the time of purchase. Additional rolled hem plates with stitch fingers of different sizes may be needed to change the stitch width.

Sewing guides (4) may be provided to guide fabric evenly while hemming or decorative stitching. They may be secured to the front of the serger or to the presser foot.

Tweezers (5) are helpful for threading a serger and are useful in areas with limited space for fingers. Hold the end of the thread with the tweezers while guiding it through the eye of a looper or needle. Tweezers are available in several styles.

Nets (6) prevent specialty threads from tangling or slipping off the spools. Use them with rayon, metallic, and parallel-wound monofilament nylon thread.

Spool caps (7) are placed directly over conventional thread spools to provide even feeding of the thread. To prevent thread snags and possible thread breakage, place the spool rim notch on the bottom.

Looper threaders (8) may be used to thread the lower looper. They are also useful for threading the eye of a needle.

Specialty presser feet are available to make certain sewing tasks easier. Similar to specialty feet for conventional sewing machines, they usually do not come with the serger at the time of purchase. Large screws secure the feet on most older serger models; most newer models use a snap-on feature that allows improved visibility for threading. Always sew test samples to determine desired results.

The **shirring foot (9)** is used to gather fabric edges or to gather the bottom piece while sewing two fabrics together. The amount of gathering is adjustable.

The **elastic tape foot (10)** guides elastics and stabilizing tapes into position while keeping them away from the knives. Most feet have an upper plate that swings out to ease elastic tape insertion and a knob to adjust the amount of consistent, applied tension.

The **cording foot (11)** has a bottom groove that guides piping between two layers of fabric. It can also be used to make your own piping.

The **blindstitch foot (12)** has a long leading edge to guide the fabric fold of a blind hem. It may be adjustable so you can match the stitch bite to the fabric weight.

The **beading foot (13)** has a top groove to guide strings of beads, pearls, sequins, etc.

The **lace foot (14)** has a long leading edge to guide the placement of laces and ribbons along the edge of the fabric.

The **gimp or yarn application foot (15)** has a small slot at the front and back to guide thin threads or wires along the cut edge of the fabric.

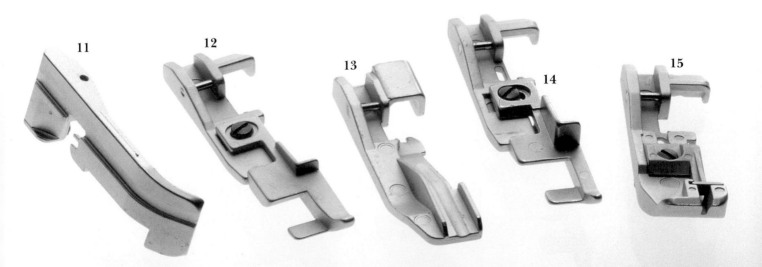

11   12   13   14   15

Buying Thread

A serger uses more thread than a conventional sewing machine, so thread companies now offer thread in cones (1), king tubes (2), and compact tubes (3). Tubes and cones have at least 1,000 yards (920 m) of thread, and cones can have as many as 6,000 yards (5520 m).

All-purpose thread may also be used on the serger; it is available on parallel-wound (4) or cross-wound (5) spools. Parallel-wound spools require the use of a spool cap (page 21) for even feeding. There is a wider color selection in all-purpose thread; use it for mediumweight or heavyweight fabrics when color-matching is critical.

Serger threads are generally lighter in weight than all-purpose sewing threads. A lightweight thread is generally recommended for serger use. There is more thread in a serged seam and a lighter-weight thread reduces bulk.

Decorative threads, including metallic thread (6), topstitching thread (7), texturized nylon (8), and lightweight ribbons (9) and yarns (10), may also be used on a serger (pages 118 and 119).

Sergers will sew with threads of 100% cotton, 100% synthetic, or cotton and synthetic blends. All these thread types work well, although cotton threads can create lint in the tension discs, and synthetics can leave a sticky residue. Although this is normal, the lint and residue must be cleaned out of the tension discs occasionally. Use the knotted-thread method (page 26) for thorough cleaning.

Determining Thread Quality

Use threads that are fine and evenly twisted with few or no loose fibers. Threads with excess fibers and uneven areas will not produce a perfect stitch. If the stitch quality cannot be improved by machine tension adjustments, change the brand or type of thread you are using. A thread may sew well on one fabric and not on another.

Serger machines sew at a higher rate of speed than conventional sewing machines and create more stress on the threads. Therefore, threads need to be strong and durable. Test thread for strength; poor-quality thread may break easily in some spots. Use the best quality of thread you can; bargain threads sometimes cause more problems than the savings are worth.

If the thread is wavy when it becomes low on the cone or spool, do not continue to use it on the serger. This wavy thread can cause stitching problems, and the seam may pucker when the garment is laundered. Save this thread for hand sewing.

Using Bobbins on a Serger

To avoid buying several spools of each color, wind thread on the bobbins of the conventional machine. Use the bobbins on the spool pins of the serger to thread the needles, where the least amount of thread is used, and use the cones to thread the loopers. If a bobbin will not fit over the spool pin, place it in a cup or glass behind the machine. As you stitch, the container will allow a free flow of the thread while the bobbin bounces around.

Blending thread colors allows stitches to blend easily with fabric. It is not always necessary to use a thread color that matches the fabric, and you may even blend several shades in the same seam. A supply of serger threads should include colors that blend easily, such as ivory, gray, or rose. Threads in the primary colors of red, yellow, and blue do not blend with many colors of fabric. If you have only one spool of matching thread, use it in the needle at the seamline, and use colors that blend for the other threads.

Organizing the Sewing Room

Sewing room organization is a major contributing factor to successful sewing. Even small spaces can yield comfortable work areas in the home.

For comfortable and productive sewing, both the serger and the conventional sewing machine should be within easy reach and placed so you can move from one machine to the other, without changing chairs. A rolling chair is a good choice; it works best on a clear mat over carpeting or on an uncarpeted floor.

Manufacturers of sewing room, computer, and general office furniture produce cabinets and tables to accommodate both machines. Corner units, which place the machines at right angles to each other, and straight-line designs, which place machines side by side, are available. There are also fold-up table units to fit either the serger or the conventional sewing machine. These units require a minimum of storage space.

Cone thread racks contribute to an organized sewing room. A selection of basic colors of serger thread should be placed near the sewing area for convenience.

Good lighting is essential. Natural light, although ideal, is not always available. Many auxiliary lamps are available, including lamps that can be clamped onto a table edge and small lamps designed to attach to the machine. Some lamps include a magnifying glass. Others provide full-spectrum lighting; they are superb task lights because they eliminate the distortion of yellow light and the irritating flicker and glare common with other bulbs.

Sewing Lamps

Adjustable arm or gooseneck lamps allow for perfect positioning of the light source.

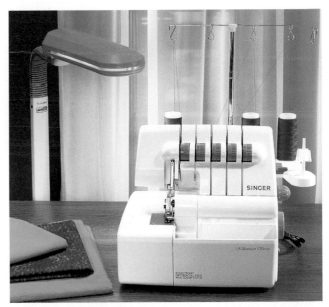

Full-spectrum lighting replicates natural sunlight to reveal true colors, and it burns cooler to save energy. It is available in a variety of table and floor lamp styles as well as portable boxes and tubes to fit most fluorescent fixtures.

Maintenance

Proper maintenance of your serger can prevent costly repairs. A regular routine of cleaning and oiling will ensure many years of trouble-free operation. Sergers need to be cleaned and oiled more frequently than conventional sewing machines because they operate at high speed and the internal parts rotate more often. Replace needles for good stitch quality, and replace knives to ensure smooth, even trimming as necessary.

Cleaning & Oiling

Serger knives create a great deal of lint, which must be cleaned from the machine frequently, using a dry lint brush.

Consult the instruction manual for instructions on oiling your serger. A pinpoint oiler, left, is especially convenient for reaching all places without dripping.

Use sewing machine oil; oil intended for household use should not be used, because it is too heavy. (If liquid fray preventer is used accidentally instead of sewing machine oil, it will have to be removed by a sewing machine service technician.)

On the average, the machine should be oiled after every eight hours of actual running or "pedal-down" time. A serger should run with a smooth, humming sound; if it does not, it needs oil. Also oil a serger that has been sitting unused for two months, because oil drains to the bottom of the machine.

Tips for Serger Maintenance

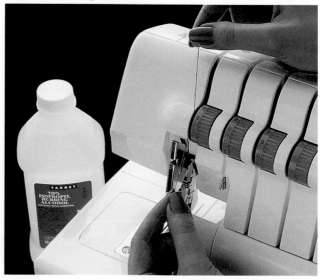

Cleaning tension discs. Tie several knots in a 6" to 10" (15 to 25.5 cm) length of buttonhole twist; soak in rubbing alcohol. Work knotted thread back and forth between tension discs several times to remove lint buildup.

Replacing Needles

Most sergers sew with a needle that has a flat shank on the back of the needle. It is similar to the type of needle a conventional sewing machine uses. Some sergers use a round-shank needle. Needles are not interchangeable. If you are unsure of the needle type your serger uses, check your instruction manual.

Serger needles wear out quickly because overlocks sew at a high speed. Needles that are dull, bent, or burred will cause stitching problems. If skipped stitches, uneven stitches, or puckered seams occur, change the needle. If the problem is not corrected, try a second new needle; a new needle is occasionally defective. Change the needle size for different fabric weights, as you do for conventional machines. If you are sewing a stitch that uses two needles, they should be the same size.

Replacing Knives

Knives wear out periodically and require replacement. They should not be sharpened. The instruction manual gives specific information on how to change knives for your model.

Sergers use a dual-blade cutting system, which has a stationary blade and a movable upper blade. The upper blade is made of a strong carbide steel and does not wear out as quickly as the lower blade, of softer steel. Carbide steel blades are more expensive than softer steel blades. While softer steel blades do need to be replaced more frequently, it is an asset to have one softer blade if a pin is accidentally hit. Then, the softer, less-expensive blade is damaged, because it gives, and the carbide blade may not be damaged at all.

During normal use, the lower blade may need to be replaced after three to six months; the upper blade may last from one to five years.

The fiber content of the fabrics you sew affects the performance of the blade. If you frequently sew synthetics, especially polyester, nylon, or spandex, you may need to replace the lower blade.

If the trimmed fabric is ragged, check the alignment of the blades. The lower blade may have slipped out of position if there has been a fabric jam, if you hit a pin accidentally, or if the set screw has loosened.

If the knives are correctly aligned and the trimmed fabric is ragged, the lower blade needs replacing. It also needs replacing if trimming causes pulled threads on lightweight fabrics.

If the fabric still does not trim neatly after a new lower blade has been correctly replaced, change the upper blade. The upper blade should also be changed whenever there is noticeable damage to the cutting edge, such as a nick.

The first time you need to replace the upper blade, take it to the dealer, and watch as the blade is correctly installed. It is very important that the upper blade be correctly aligned with the lower blade; if incorrectly positioned, it can cause either jammed fabric or damage to the blades.

Replacing a round-shank needle. Insert new needle as far as it will go, with long groove on needle toward the front. Insert point of another needle into the eye; rotate it until parallel to needle plate for proper alignment. Tighten set screw.

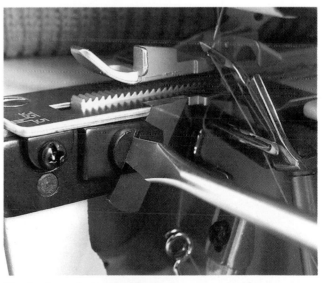

Replacing a lower knife. Raise upper knife. Loosen set screw; remove lower knife. Insert new knife so top of blade is level with needle plate. Tighten set screw. Rotate handwheel several times before sewing on fabric to mesh cutting edges of blades and to remove any uneven areas on new blade.

Basic Serger Techniques

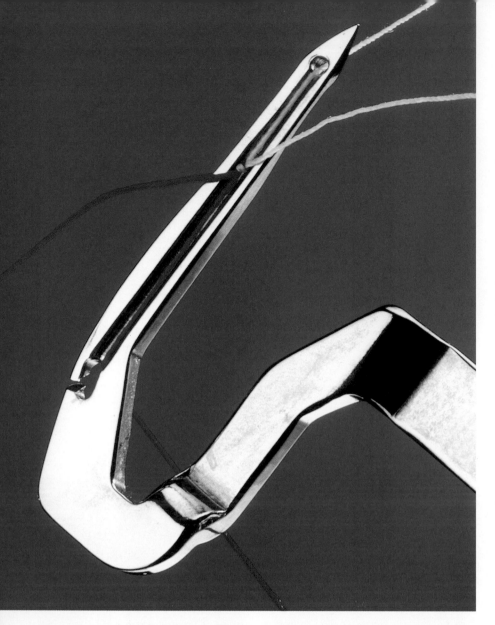

Threading a Serger

Threading a serger appears to be complicated at first, but with practice it is not difficult. An easy method for threading a serger is the tying-on method. Simply cut the old threads and tie on new ones; then pull each new thread through the machine, using the tail of the old thread.

When a thread breaks, or if the machine is run until a spool is empty, it is necessary to thread the serger manually. Carefully place each thread in the proper path, following the threading guide in the instruction manual or on the door of the serger. It is important that the machine be threaded correctly, or it will not stitch correctly. Consult your dealer if you have questions.

Check the threading of the serger whenever it does not stitch correctly; a thread may not be in all the thread guides, or threads may be tangled. Be sure the thread stand is completely extended and that a thread is not caught around the thread stand, under a spool, or on a thread guide.

Tips for Manual Threading

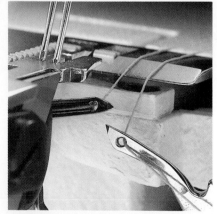

Rotate handwheel until loopers are positioned so they do not cross, before threading lower looper. If lower looper is threaded when it crosses upper looper, threads will tangle, and serger will not stitch.

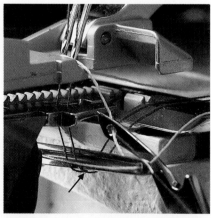

Thread needles last. If needles are threaded before loopers, needle threads (blue) loop under lower looper and become trapped (arrow), and serger will not stitch unless you draw threads above needle plate, as shown at right.

Draw threads above the needle plate, using tweezers or seam ripper, before stitching if needles are threaded before loopers; this prevents tangling.

How to Thread a Serger Using the Tying-on Method

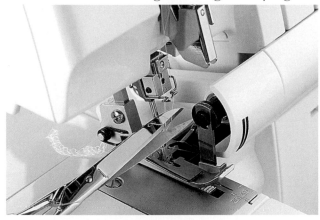

1) Clip threads just in front of the needles. (Your machine may have only one needle.)

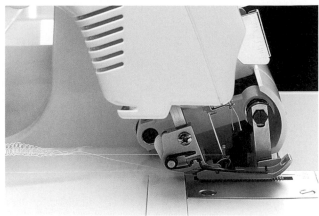

2) Hold tail chain, and run machine slowly until you have 3" to 4" (7.5 to 10 cm) of straight threads behind the presser foot. (A chain will not form because the needles are not threaded.)

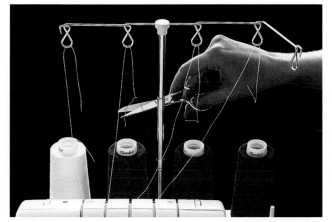

3) Cut threads close to spools on thread stand. Place new threads on stand. Tie new and old threads together. Clip threads 1" (2.5 cm) from knot; if you clip tails close to knot, threads may come untied.

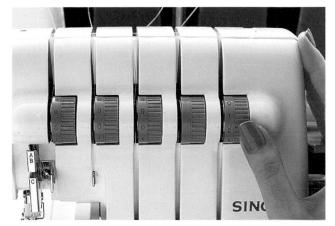

4) Lift presser foot to release tension of needle threads. Note positions of looper tension dials, if desired, and turn each to "0".

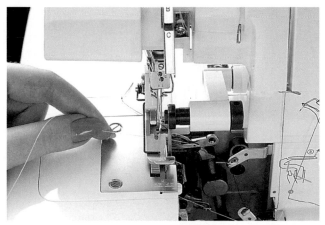

5) Pull one tied-on looper thread through machine, pulling gently from behind presser foot. If thread does not pull easily, check whether it is caught on a thread guide or wrapped around a thread stand. Pull each thread through the machine, one at a time.

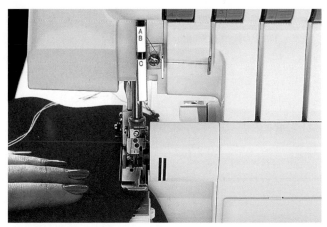

6) Return tension dials to desired settings. Thread needles after cutting off knots. Bring all threads under, and slightly to the left of, presser foot. Lower presser foot. Run fabric scraps under the foot to check tension; adjust tension, if necessary.

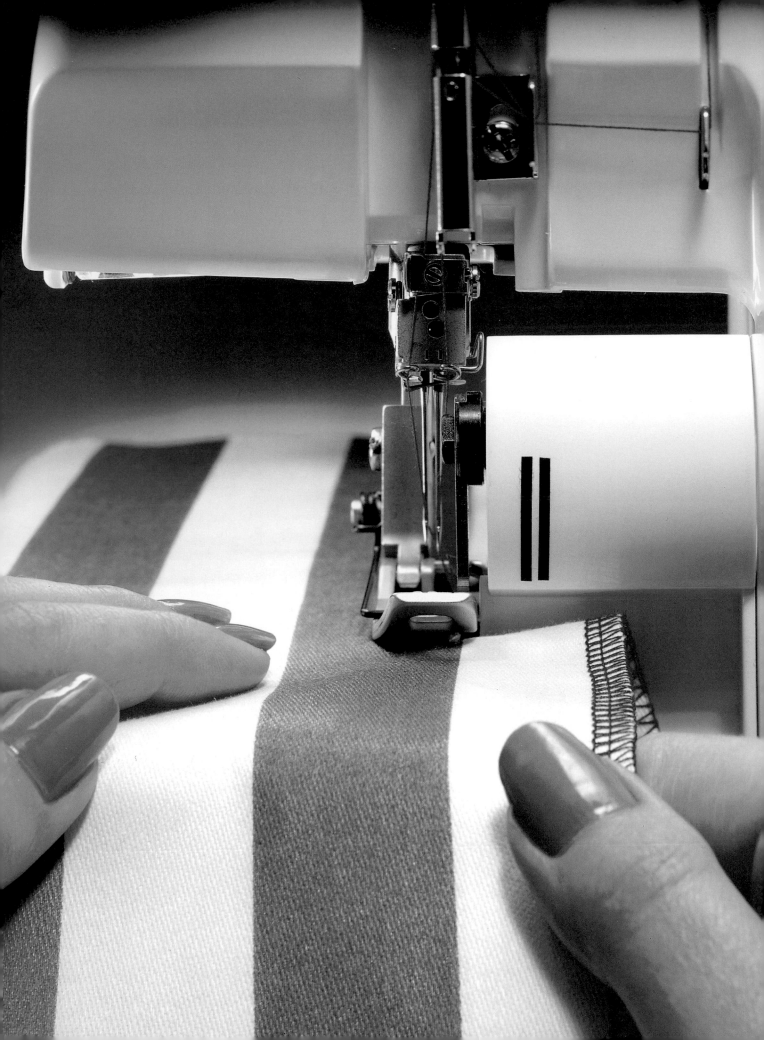

Basic Techniques

The serger is designed so the knives will trim the fabric just before the needle and loopers form the stitches. When operating a serger, watch the knives instead of the needle. Sewing mistakes are easy to correct; trimming mistakes are not.

Allow the knives to trim the fabric slightly, even if you are sewing a seam finish, so there will be a neat raw edge for the machine to overedge. A seam allowance that has started to ravel is irregular; if it is not trimmed by the knives, the stitches will be uneven in appearance.

Practice sewing on scraps before sewing garments to become familiar with exactly where the knife blades are and how they work. You may want to use a striped fabric. Learn to guide the fabric so you trim exactly on one of the stripes. Then become familiar with the needle placement, guiding the striped fabric so you stitch exactly on a stripe.

When seams are serged, the needle stitches on the seamline. (For a machine with two needles, the left needle stitches on the seamline.) When ⅝" (1.5 cm) seam allowances are allowed, stitch so the left needle is ⅝" (1.5 cm) from the edge of the fabric. The knives will automatically trim off the correct amount.

Tips for Guiding Fabric

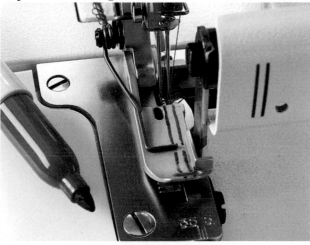

Mark front of presser foot directly in front of each needle, using permanent marking pen. Guide fabric, positioning seamline at mark. When sewing with two needles, use mark for left needle.

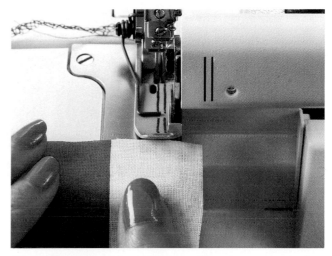

Use narrow graphic tape or masking tape, marked at various widths, on looper cover to guide raw edge of fabric.

Practice trimming with the knives by sewing along one of the stripes in a striped fabric until you can trim evenly and accurately.

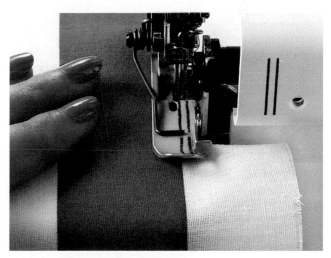

Practice guiding fabric along one of the stripes in a striped fabric, so needle stitches exactly on a stripe.

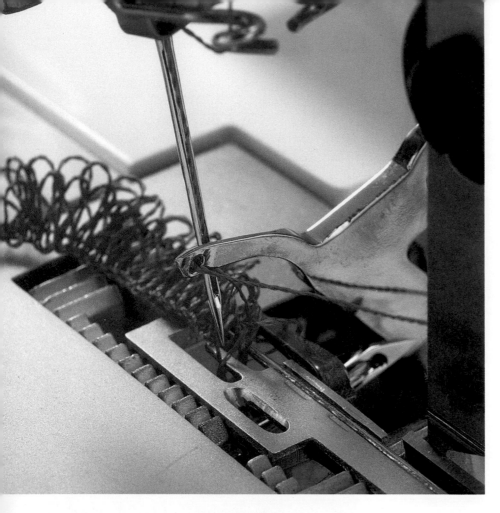

Clearing the Stitch Fingers

The serger forms its stitches around one or two stitch fingers located on the needle plate, as shown at left. Occasionally, it is necessary to remove the stitches from the needle plate; this is referred to as clearing the stitch fingers.

Clear the stitch fingers before changing the needle plate on the serger. Also, when you turn outside corners, the stitch fingers must be cleared because stitches are always left chained around the stitch fingers at the end of the seam.

How to Clear the Stitch Fingers

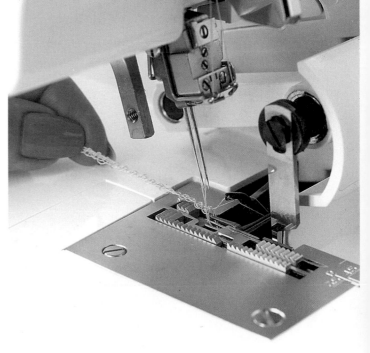

1) Lift the presser foot, and raise the needle or needles. Pull about ½" (1.3 cm) of slack in each needle thread just above needles.

2) Pull on tail chain to release stitches from stitch fingers. Correct amount of slack pulled in needle threads, step 1, allows tail chain to barely slide off stitch fingers. (Presser foot has been removed to show detail.)

Avoiding Common Problems

To avoid loop. Do not pull too much slack in the needle threads at the end of seam.

To avoid extra threads. Stop right at the edge of the fabric. If you stitch a few stitches beyond the edge, there will be extra threads at the end of the seam.

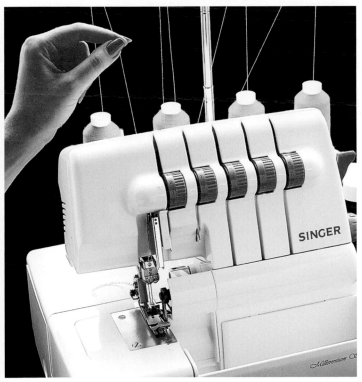

3) Tug on all threads near telescope until threads are taut, if too much slack has been pulled.

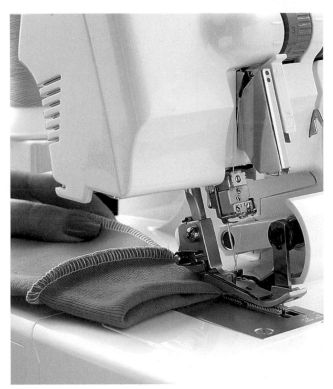

End of a seam. Lift presser foot and pull slack in needle threads as in step 1, opposite. Pull back on fabric to release stitches from stitch fingers.

Securing Tail Chains

In garment construction, tail chains are trimmed away at intersecting seams, as on page 56. T-shirts serged using the flat method of construction and garments with a prefinished hemline, such as an eyelet border or scalloped lace, will require the tail chain to be secured so it does not show at the end of a seam.

Because sergers cannot back-stitch, keep stitches from raveling by using one of several methods for securing tail chains. An easy method uses a tapestry needle to hide the tail chain, left. For this method, you may want to smooth out the loops in the tail chain, using your fingers, before thread-ing the tail chain through the large eye of a tapestry needle. Weave the needle under the over-locked stitches for 1" to 2" (2.5 to 5 cm). Cut off the rest of the tail chain for a neat finish.

You may use a loop turner to secure the tail chain, or secure the stitches at the end of the seam with liquid fray preventer. While these methods are easy, they require more time than the serger method, opposite.

How to Secure Tail Chains Using Liquid Fray Preventer or Loop Turner

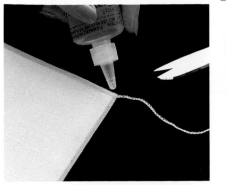

Liquid fray preventer. Apply liquid fray preventer to stitches at end of seam. Allow to dry; cut tail chain close to stitches.

Loop turner. 1) Smooth out loops in tail chain, using fingers. Insert loop turner under stitches 1" or 2" (2.5 to 5 cm) from end of seam. Catch ends of tail chain with latch hook of loop turner.

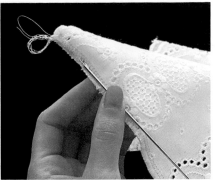

2) Pull tail chain under stitches, using loop turner. Cut off excess tail chain.

How to Secure Tail Chains Using the Serger

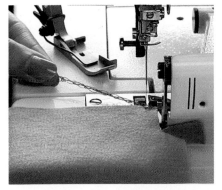

Starting a seam. 1) Stitch seam for one or two stitches. Raise presser foot and needle. Clear stitch fingers (pages 34 and 35). Run fingers along tail chain to smooth out loops. (Presser foot has been removed to show detail.)

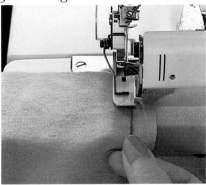

2) Bring tail chain to the left, around and under presser foot. Place tail chain between needle and knives. Lower presser foot, holding tail chain in position.

3) Stitch seam over tail chain for about 1" (2.5 cm). Then, swing tail chain to the right, so it is trimmed off as you continue to stitch seam.

Ending a seam. 1) Stitch past end of seam by one stitch; stop. Raise presser foot and needle to clear stitch fingers (pages 34 and 35). (Presser foot has been removed to show detail.)

2) Turn fabric over, and align edge of seam with trimming edge of knives. Lower presser foot. Turn handwheel to insert needle at end of seam and to the left of trimmed edge, the width of stitch.

3) Stitch over previous stitching for about 1" (2.5 cm). Stitch off edge, leaving tail chain. Using scissors or knives, cut tail chain close to edge of seam.

Curves & Corners

Special methods are used for stitching curves, such as facings, necklines, and armholes, and corners, such as kick pleats and plackets. When you are sewing curves, the long presser foot prevents the fabric from being turned abruptly. Differential feed (page 46) may be used to prevent stretching the fabric along bias-cut edges. On inside corners, the knives trim up to the corner before the needle stitches to it. And on outside corners, fabric cannot be pivoted, because threads are chained around the stitch fingers.

Practice these methods, shown below, on trial scraps of fabric; then serge placemats and napkins as a fast and easy project.

How to Stitch a Curved Edge

Outside curve. 1) Increase differential feed slightly, if desired, to ease fabric and reduce overstretching seam. Begin trimming at an angle, until desired trimming or stitching position is reached.

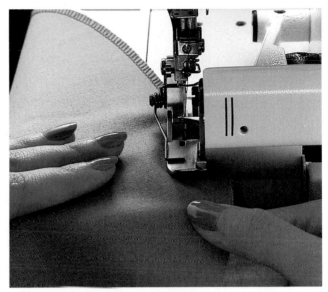

2) Stitch, guiding fabric by moving it to the right in front of presser foot; watch knives, not needle. Lift presser foot as necessary on tight curves to ease fabric under presser foot.

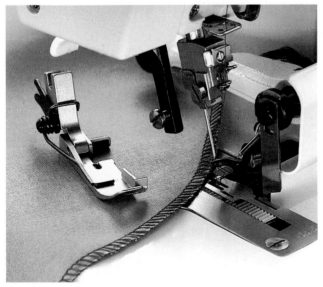

3) Overlap previous stitches for circular edges. Stop, and lift presser foot. Shift fabric so it is behind the needle; stitch straight off edge to prevent gradual looping over edge. (Presser foot has been removed to show needle position.)

Inside curve. Trim and stitch as for outside curve, above, guiding fabric by moving it to the left in front of presser foot. On circular edges, stitch off edge of fabric (page 57).

How to Stitch an Outside Corner

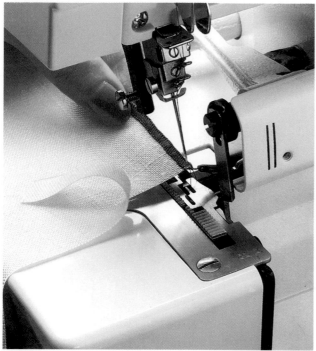

1) Stitch one side of fabric, trimming as desired; stop a few inches (centimeters) before corner. Trim away seam allowance on adjacent side for about 2" (5 cm). Or, cut fabric to finished size. Sew one stitch past end of the corner, and clear stitch fingers (pages 34 and 35). (Presser foot has been removed to show detail.)

2) Pivot the fabric; align edge of trimmed seam allowance with knives. Insert needle at edge. Lower presser foot, and continue stitching. Stitches will overlap at corner. (Presser foot has been removed to show needle position.)

Alternate method. 1) Stitch one side of fabric. Start trimming adjacent side with knives; stop serging when needle takes first stitch on fabric. With needle down, lift presser foot and straighten corner by pulling fabric to the left at right angle.

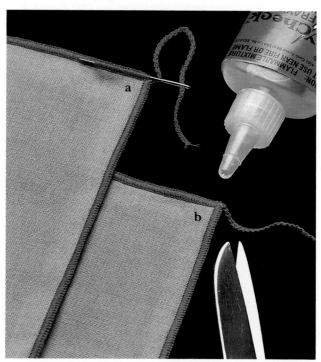

2) Lower presser foot; overlock, leaving 4" (10 cm) tail chains at ends. Secure tail chains (pages 36 and 37) by threading them under stitches using needle **(a)**; or by applying liquid fray preventer **(b)** at corners.

How to Stitch an Inside Corner or Slit

1) **Finish** seams by aligning raw edge of fabric with knives of serger. Stitch, stopping when knives reach the corner or slit.

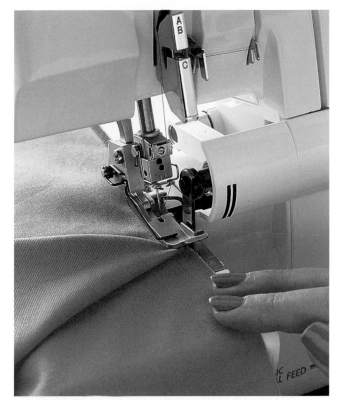

2a) **Stitch** inside corner, folding fabric to left to straighten edge. Stitch through corner; hold fabric in straight line. Once past corner, fabric can be relaxed.

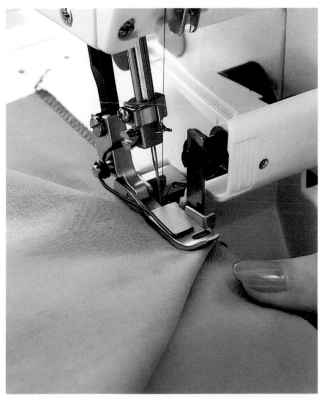

2b) **Stitch** slit by straightening edge of fabric; fold two folds to distribute fullness. Stitch, holding fabric in straight line.

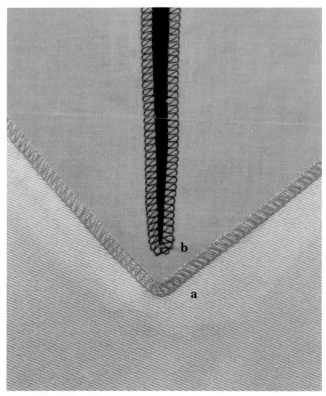

3) **Press** completed inside corner (**a**) or slit (**b**) flat. (Folds in step 2a or 2b are not caught in stitching.)

Removing Stitches & Jammed Fabric

Even if you are an experienced sewer, you may have to rip out stitches occasionally. Serger stitches look intricate, but they are actually easy to remove. Also, fabric may not feed through the serger properly, causing a fabric jam. If a fabric jam occurs, the fabric can be removed safely from the machine without damage.

Removing Stitches, Restitching Seams

There are times when ripping stitches is unavoidable. After the stitches have been removed, remember that the excess seam allowance has already been trimmed away. When restitching the seam, guide the fabric along the left edge of the knives.

If the seam needs to be deeper, it is not always necessary to remove the stitches first. When the fabric is lightweight and bulky seam allowances are a concern, remove the stitches. Otherwise, sew the new seam and trim away the original stitches in one step.

Removing Jammed Fabric

Thick fabrics that do not feed into the small opening of the knife blades may cause the fabric to bunch up at the knives. The fabric can be compressed prior to sewing with the serger by stitching along the edge of the fabric on a conventional machine, using a straight or zigzag stitch. Fabric jams also occur when the stitch length is too short. Gradually lengthen the stitch until the fabric feeds through the serger as desired.

When a tail chain becomes tangled in the stitching or in the moving parts of the machine, the fabric will jam under the presser foot. This is most likely to occur in stitches including the chainstitch. Always bring tail chains over the presser foot to cut them with the knives, and leave a tail chain at least 4" (10 cm) long. Also, do not allow trimmings to fall into the machine; they may catch on the loopers and cause a jam.

Remove a fabric jam carefully to avoid damaging the fabric or changing the machine's timing. Pulling hard or yanking on the jammed fabric can also bend the loopers, but it does not release the jam. It is important that you stop sewing as soon as you realize the fabric is not feeding into your serger well and a fabric jam is starting to occur.

There are two methods for removing fabric jams. If it is possible to rotate the handwheel and raise the needles, follow the instructions for the needle-up method (page 45). In a more serious fabric jam, the needle cannot be raised; follow the instructions for the needle-down method (page 45).

How to Remove Chainstitches

1) **Pull** looper thread out of the last loop in the stitch at the end of the seam, using a pin; work from the underside of the fabric.

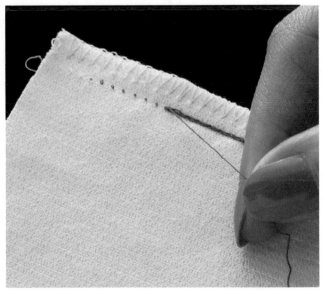

2) **Bring** needle thread through to upper side of fabric; gently pull looper thread to unravel stitches. Remove the loose needle thread.

How to Remove Overlock Stitches

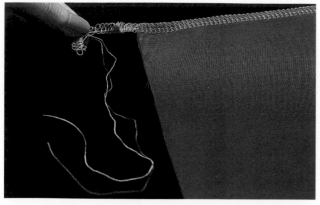

1) Locate the thread for each needle by smoothing out the loops in the tail chain. The needle threads are the shortest threads in the chain. (For 2-thread or 3-thread stitches, there is only one needle thread.)

2) Hold the needle threads, and push the excess tail chain stitches close to the fabric at the end of the seam.

3) Pull the needle threads, gently easing the fabric until the needle threads can be removed.

4) Remove the looper threads.

Alternate method. Cut one of the looper threads by sliding a seam ripper along the stitches. Pull remaining needle and looper threads out of the fabric.

How to Remove Cover Stitches

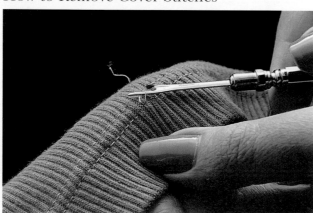

1) Remove the last two or three stitches formed by each of the needle threads, using a pin or seam ripper. If it is difficult to determine the last stitch, as it may be in a circular hem, remove the stitches to the right of the overlapped stitches.

2) Turn the fabric over and gently pull on the looper thread until all stitches are unraveled. Remove the loose needle threads. Remove remaining circular hem stitches, if necessary.

How to Remove a Fabric Jam (needle up)

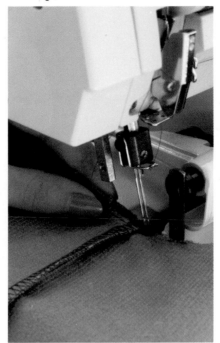

1) Cut the needle threads. Remove the presser foot.

2) Tug gently on fabric, pulling to the back of the machine. If fabric does not come out easily, cut the looper threads close to the fabric.

3) Pull fabric from machine gently. Use seam ripper to remove stitches from the fabric. Rethread serger; replace presser foot.

How to Remove a Fabric Jam (needle down)

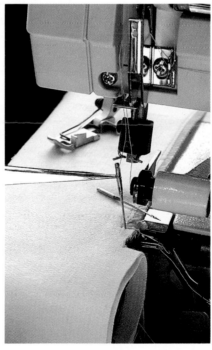

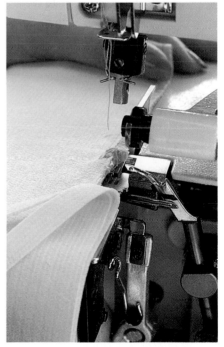

1) Loosen the needle set screws. Raise the needle bar by turning the handwheel. (Needles will remain in the fabric.)

2) Remove the presser foot. Cut needle and looper threads close to fabric. Pull needle out of fabric using tweezers or fingers.

3) Pull fabric to back of machine to remove it. Use a seam ripper to remove stitches from the fabric. Remove threads from under lower looper, if necessary. Insert new needle. Rethread serger; replace presser foot.

Differential Feed

All sewing machines depend on feed dogs to grip the fabric and move it under the presser foot. The differential feed system, available on most sergers, uses two sets of feed dogs to allow change in fabric movement; the front feed dogs deliver fabric to the needle, and the back feed dogs move the fabric away after the stitches are formed. Differential feed can be adjusted to prevent both puckering and overstretching of fabric. It can also be used to gather fabric. The results are more consistent than when the same things are controlled by hand.

Feed dogs normally move the fabric into and away from the needles at the same pace. This normal, 1:1 ratio setting is sometimes referred to as "1" on the differential feed control lever. Adjusting the lever changes the way the front feed dogs work.

When the differential feed control lever is moved to a smaller number, or stretch, the front feed dogs push less fabric toward the needle while the back feed dogs continue to carry away the same amount. Puckers, a common problem when sewing some slippery or very lightweight fabrics, disappear; the fabric, under slight tension when the stitches are formed, relaxes as it comes off the back of the serger. The smaller setting may also improve stitch quality when serging rolled hems, and it may increase some stretched effects, such as the lettuce hem (page 62).

When the differential feed control lever is moved to a larger number, or gather, the front feed dogs push more fabric toward the needle than the back feed dogs carry away, and extra fabric is included in each stitch. A setting slightly larger than normal will ease the fabric so wavy seams or edges, caused by stretching bias-cut edges, loosely wovens, or knits, are eliminated. Fabric layers can be eased or gathered together; for example, the back shoulder may be eased to the front shoulder, or a ruffle may be gathered while serging the seam. The largest differential feed control setting will gather many fabrics to about half the original length.

Test-sew before serging projects. Longer stitch length, lighter fabric weight, and softer fabric body will increase the effects. Also, practice changing the differential feed to a larger number as you serge around curves; practice returning to a normal setting as the curves straighten.

Differential feed makes gathering smooth, even ruffles fast and easy.

How Differential Feed Controls Vary

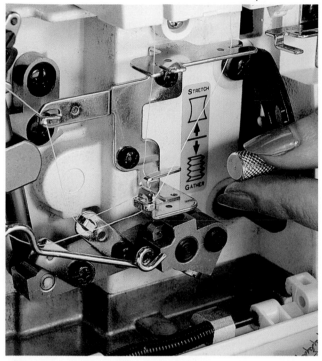

The differential feed control lever may be located behind the looper cover. Stretch and gather adjustments may be illustrated.

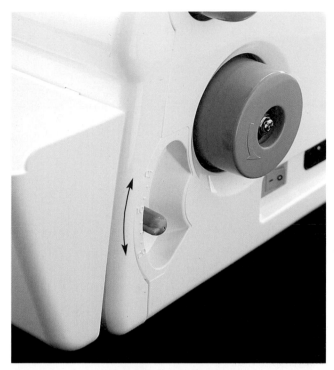

On some serger models, the differential feed control lever is located on the side of the machine, for easier access. Adjustments may correspond numerically to the normal 1:1 feed ratio; larger numbers gather fabric.

How to Gather Fabric Using Differential Feed

Single Layer. Adjust differential feed for gathering; use shirring foot, if desired. Serge near edge of fabric, trimming slightly. Serger gathers fabric automatically.

How to Ease or Gather Layers Together

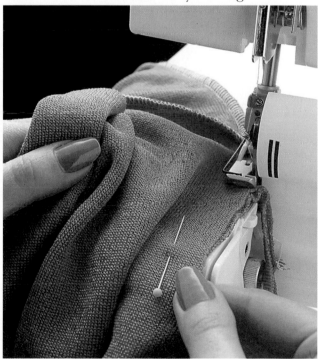

Adjust differential feed to ease or gather as desired; use shirring foot, if desired. Place longer fabric layer next to feed dogs, beneath shorter fabric layer. For example, the sleeve cap is placed beneath the armhole to ease a smooth seam.

Seams & Seam Finishes

Serged seams can be used on many garments. Your instruction manual may include suggestions for where stitches are used. Garment style, fabric selection, and personal preference will help you decide which seams to use. The serged seam alone is not always suitable for garment construction. Many seams are sewn using both the serger and the conventional machine. For example, pants, jackets, or garments requiring adjustable fit, or seams that will be subjected to a great amount of stress, should be sewn with a pressed-open conventional seam and overedged seam allowances.

Types of Seams & Seam Finishes

Overlock seams (pages 16 and 17) are appropriate for wovens and knits. Choose the 3-thread overlock for loosely fitted or nonstressed seams. The more secure 4-thread and 5-thread safety stitches are used primarily for wovens because the chainstitch may pop when stretched. The 3-thread and 4-thread mock safety stitches, designed for durable stretch seams, may also be used on wovens.

Overedge seam finish (page 50) for conventional seams is used when it is desirable to keep the entire 5/8" (1.5 cm) seam allowance. It is the best choice for tailored garments sewn from wools, linens, and silk suitings. It is also recommended whenever fit is uncertain to allow for letting out seams.

Reinforced seam (page 50) is recommended for seams that will be stressed.

French seam (page 50) is used for sheers and loosely woven fabrics. The seam will add bulk, so it is best used on full, gathered items like skirts and curtains.

Rolled seam (page 50) may be used instead of French seams for sheers that are firmly woven and for laces.

Mock flat-fell seam (page 50) is used for denim and other heavyweight woven fabrics.

Reversible lapped seam (page 51) is used for reversible garments or for thick, loosely woven fabrics to provide added strength.

Gathered seam (page 51) is finished in one easy step using differential feed and a shirring foot. An alternate method uses the conventional machine with the serger.

Mock flatlock seam (page 52) is used for a decorative effect, with decorative thread used in the upper looper.

Flatlock on a fold (page 52) is used for the decorative effect of a flatlock seam on fabric that has been folded and stitched.

Types of Stabilized Seams

There are several methods for stabilizing seams in serger garment construction. The type of fabric you are sewing and the desired effect will determine which method you choose.

Fusible stabilized seam (page 53) uses fusible interfacing strips to stabilize seams. Interfacing can also be used as a stable base for decorative edge finishes on stretchy knit or bias-cut fabrics.

Elastic stabilized seam (page 53) uses transparent elastic to allow full stretch and recovery in a serged seam, but prevents fabric from stretching out of shape.

Nonstretch stabilized seam (page 53) uses twill tape, seam tape, or ribbon to prevent stretching of the fabric at the seamline.

Slight-stretch stabilized seam (page 53) uses tricot bias binding to reinforce and stabilize a seam where slight stretch is desired. Use this method for stabilizing seams in sweater knits and T-shirt knits, which need support without completely restricting the stretch of the fabric.

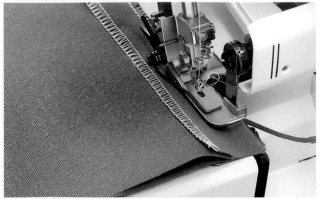

Overedge seam finish for conventional seam. Stitch 5⁄8" (1.5 cm) seam, right sides together, using conventional machine. Stitch seam allowances, slightly trimming raw edge, using overedge or overlock stitch.

Reinforced seam. Stitch 5⁄8" (1.5 cm) seam, right sides together, using conventional machine; use narrow zigzag on moderate-stretch knits. Serge seam allowances together 1⁄8" (3 mm) from seamline.

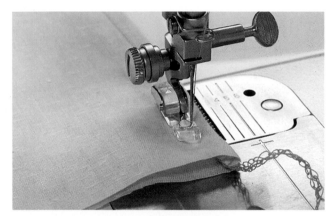

French seam. Overedge seam, wrong sides together, with left needle positioned 1⁄4" (6 mm) inside seam allowance. Fold fabric, right sides together, enclosing overedged fabric; press. Straight-stitch close to enclosed stitches, using zipper foot on the conventional machine.

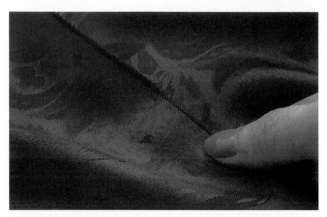

Rolled seam. Place fabric right sides together. Stitch seam, using a rolled hem stitch (pages 79 to 81), with needle positioned on seamline; trim excess seam allowance. Press. Use tricot bias binding to stabilize lace edge, as shown on page 53, if desired.

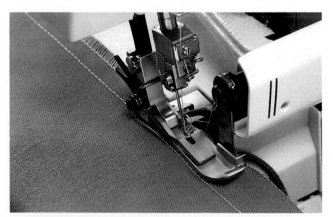

Mock flat-fell seam. 1) Place fabric right sides together. Stitch, using a conventional machine. Serge seam allowances together, trimming slightly.

2) Press seam allowance toward one side; topstitch from right side next to seamline, using a conventional machine. Topstitch again, 1⁄4" (6 mm) away, through all layers.

How to Sew a Reversible Lapped Seam

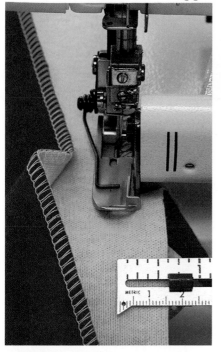

1) Stitch each single-layer seam allowance, using overedge or overlock stitch and aligning needle to seamline.

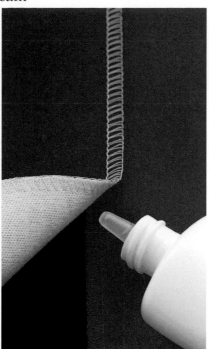

2) Lap garment sections so seamlines meet; glue-baste.

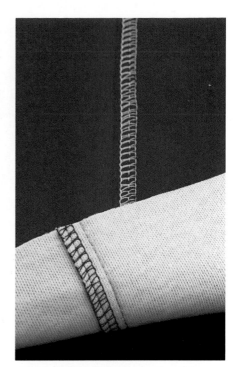

3) Straight-stitch through all layers ⅛" (3 mm) from serged stitches, from both sides of garment, using conventional machine.

How to Sew a Gathered Seam

1) Replace regular presser foot with shirring foot; set differential feed (page 46) to a larger number. Align edges of two fabric layers together; position layers so fabric to be gathered is on the bottom. Overlock the seam with needle positioned on the seamline.

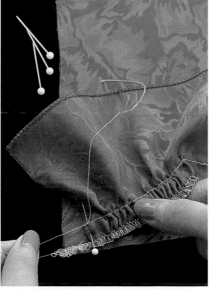

Alternate method. 1) Baste in seam allowance near seamline, using conventional machine. Overedge seam allowance, slightly trimming raw edge. Align overedged fabric to corresponding section, right sides together, matching as necessary; pin. Pull bobbin thread and serger needle thread, gathering fabric to fit.

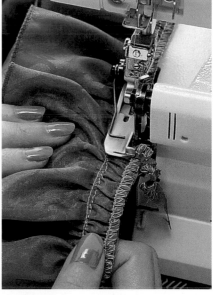

2) Stitch seam, using conventional machine. Overedge seam allowances, using serger. Or, overlock seam, with left needle positioned on seamline, trimming away excess seam allowance; remove pins as they approach knives.

How to Sew a Mock Flatlock Seam

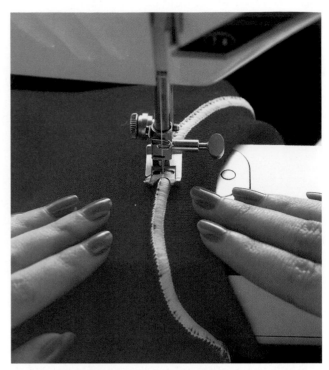

1) Use decorative thread (pages 118 and 119) in upper looper. Serge fabric, wrong sides together; press seam to one side with decorative thread on top.

2) Topstitch decorative serged seam through all layers, using conventional machine.

How to Flatlock on a Fold of Fabric

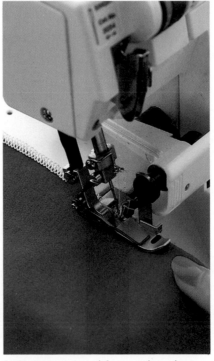

1) Mark stitch placement line on right side of fabric. Fold, *wrong* sides together, on marked line. Adjust serger for flatlock stitch (pages 74 to 77). Place fabric slightly to the left of knives.

2) Serge seam without trimming fold of fabric. Position stitches half on and half off fabric.

3) Open the fabric, and pull the stitches flat.

Stabilized Seams

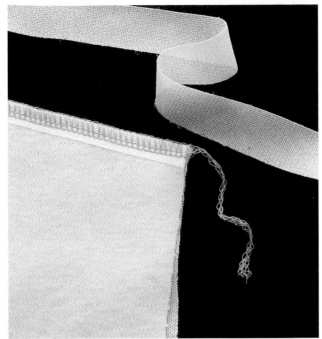

Fusible stabilized seam. Cut ¾" (2 cm) strip of fusible knit interfacing the length of the seam. Fuse to wrong side of garment. Stitch seam.

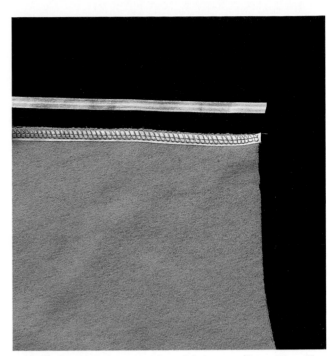

Elastic stabilized seam. Use elastic tape foot, if available; adjust foot tension to drag slightly against elastic. Serge seam, stitching through elastic; elastic should not gather seam. If using regular presser foot, place elastic over seamline and serge without trimming elastic; increase differential feed to ease fabric, if desired.

Nonstretch stabilized seam. Serge as in elastic stabilized seam, above; use twill tape, seam tape, or ribbon, and adjust foot tension so it does not drag on stabilizer. Decrease differential feed slightly, if desired, to prevent puckering of seam.

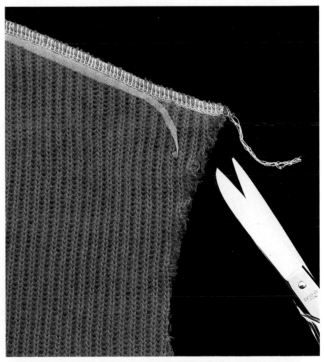

Slight-stretch stabilized seam. Cut ¾" (2 cm) strip of tricot bias binding the length of the seam. Serge through relaxed strip; trim excess binding close to stitches. Increase differential feed slightly, if desired, to ease fabric and prevent overstretching seam.

Basting Seams

Thread-basting seams to check the fit of a garment is more important when sewing with a serger than when sewing with a conventional machine because a serger trims away most of the seam allowance. Pin-basting seams is helpful to align long seam lengths, or when design details, such as tucks or pleats, need to be secured before sewing.

You may choose to baste seams on a conventional machine by using a basting stitch or a long stitch length. The 2-thread chainstitch, available on many serger models, is an alternative method that is fast and easy to remove from most fabrics (page 43). It is important to disengage the knives when basting on a serger; follow the directions in your machine manual.

When basting with pins, use as few pins as possible to reduce the risk of damaging the serger or its knives. If a pin is hit by the knives, one or both knives may need to be replaced, and the timing may need to be serviced professionally. Be especially careful to remove each pin as it approaches the knives. For loosely woven or bulky fabrics, use large pins, such as quilting pins; short, fine pins can get lost in the fabric.

Tips for Pin-basting Seams

Place pins vertically to the left of the presser foot to eliminate the risk of hitting them with the knives.

Place pins horizontally to secure tucks, pleats, or other details; remove pins as they approach knives.

Sewing Seams

In garment construction, one seam is usually stitched and then intersected by another seam or seam finish. For example, the side seam of a skirt is stitched and then intersected by seams at the waistline and hem. When one seam is intersected by another, the tail chain at the end of the first seam is trimmed away by the second seam. For fragile fabrics or seams that will be stressed, the stitches at the intersecting seams can be reinforced, as shown above. Instructions for this method are on page 56.

Sewing On & Off

When serging seams or seam finishes, you may sometimes need to overlap beginning and ending stitches. This can occur on circular edges, such as a neckline or the lower edge of a skirt, or when you have removed stitches for part of a seam, and the seam needs restitching.

One fast way to begin stitching circular edges is to stitch gradually onto the fabric at an angle; if you want to trim seam or hem allowances, stitch onto the fabric at an angle until you have cut into the edge of fabric as far as desired. Then straighten the fabric and continue stitching and trimming parallel to the edge. To stop sewing, you can simply stitch gradually toward the edge at an angle. Run about 3" (7.5 cm) of tail chain after stitching, as usual. When stitches are overlapped for 1" (2.5 cm), the tail chain may be trimmed close to stitching.

Another method is to clear the stitch fingers and lower the needle into the fabric at the seamline. This method is sometimes preferred because it prevents the gradual looping of threads over the edge of the fabric. You may use this method for restitching an area of a seam or for seams and hem finishes that do not require trimming away fabric.

You may want to practice these techniques (shown on pages 56 and 57) on scraps of fabric a few times to gain confidence before sewing garments.

How to Sew a Seam

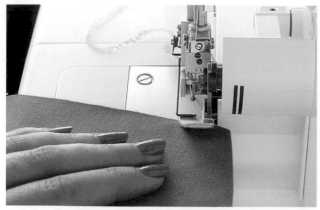

1) **Run** 2" to 3" (5 to 7.5 cm) tail chain. Place garment pieces, right sides together, under front of presser foot; it is not necessary to lift presser foot.

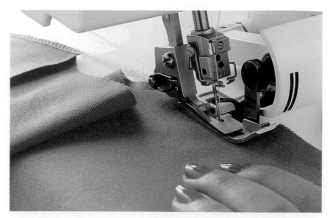

2) **Guide** fabric as you serge seam. Chainstitch multiple seams; start another seam directly behind end of completed seam without stopping the serger.

3) **Run** 4" to 6" (10 to 15 cm) tail chain on last seam. Cut tail chain, using serger's thread cutter, or scissors. Or, bring tail chain over front of presser foot and cut with knives, as shown.

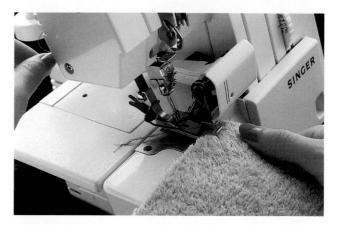

Alternate method. Run 2" to 3" (5 to 7.5 cm) tail chain. Lift presser foot. Place layers that shift under presser foot up to knives; lift leading edge of presser foot from left side if fabric is especially thick. Lower presser foot. Serge seam and cut tail chain as above.

How to Sew Intersecting Seams

Intersecting seam. Trim tail chain with knives as you stitch across an intersecting seamline. Reinforce narrow seams, if desired, using conventional straight stitch at intersection.

**Reinforced intersecting ⁵⁄₈"
(1.5 cm) seam. 1)** Stop before you meet a previous seam. Clip into seam allowance for ¼" to ⅜" (6 mm to 1 cm) on each side of stitches.

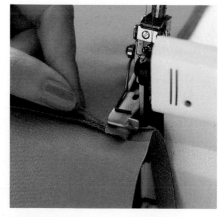

2) **Fold** clipped seam allowance away from knives, toward seam. Continue sewing past previous seam, not cutting the folded seam allowance.

How to Sew Circular Edges

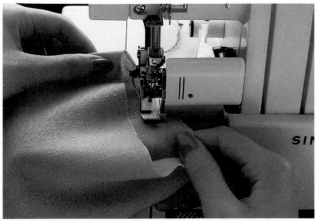

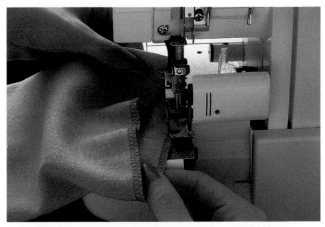

1) Stitch onto edge of fabric at an angle. Straighten fabric in front of knives as you sew. Stitch parallel to edge of fabric.

2) Overlap previous stitches for 1" (2.5 cm). Stitch off edge of fabric at an angle or by clearing stitch fingers, as in either step 2, below.

How to Restitch Part of a Seam

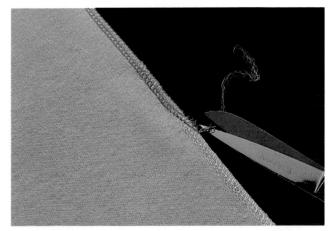

1) Stitch onto edge of fabric at an angle, starting back 2" (5 cm) from end of previous stitching. Straighten fabric when needle enters fabric exactly on previous seamline to prevent a dip at seamline.

2) Sew to end of area to be restitched; overlap stitching 1" (2.5 cm). Stitch off the edge of fabric at an angle. Trim the tail chain close to stitching. (Contrasting thread has been used to show detail.)

Alternate method. 1) Clear stitch fingers (pages 34 and 35). Place fabric under presser foot, lowering needle into fabric at seamline, so stitches will overlap previous stitching 1" (2.5 cm). Lower presser foot.

2) Sew to end of area to be restitched; overlap stitching 1" (2.5 cm). Clear stitch fingers. Run tail chain, and trim close to stitching.

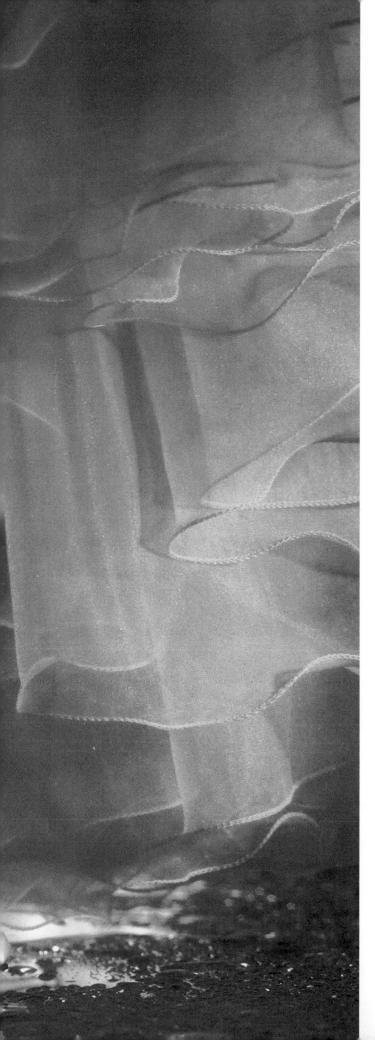

Hems

Sergers create professional hem finishes on sheers, knits, or wovens. A serger may be used for sewing hems on all types of garments, from sportswear to evening wear. In some cases, the serger is used with the conventional sewing machine.

Overedged and blindstitched hem (page 60) reduces bulk by using an overedged finish instead of hem tape or a double-fold hem.

Overedged and topstitched hem (page 60) has an overedged finish with the addition of conventional machine topstitching to imitate the cover stitch hem.

Eased hem (page 60) is used on mediumweight to heavyweight fabric for flared or full hems.

Blind hem (page 60) is used for hems on many fabrics; it works best on textured knits because stitches will not show.

Cover stitch hem (page 61) simultaneously finishes the fabric edge and secures the hem in place with double topstitching.

Sport hem (page 61) is used for a decorative application on sweatshirt fleece or T-shirt fabric.

Fringed hem (page 61) uses a decorative flatlock stitch for detailing on scarves, shawls, and table linens.

Rolled hem (page 62) can be used to finish edges of scarves, ruffles, table linens, and some garments. It is suitable for lightweight to mediumweight fabrics, such as sheers, silkies, and broadcloth.

Lettuce hem (page 62) ripples the edge of knits or bias-cut wovens for a decorative finish with a feminine touch. Often seen on children's and T-shirt neckline ribbing, it is also used on swimwear, aerobic wear, and evening wear.

Fishline hem (page 62) adds firmness and body to lightweight fabric flounces and ruffles. Fishline, 8-pound-test to 10-pound-test, provides supple curls, as shown at left; 25-pound-test is more firm. This hem is often used to embellish costumes and evening wear.

Wire hem (page 62) gives fabrics a stiff, shapable edge. A 24-gauge floral wire is commonly used to make decorative ribbons.

Shirt-tail hem (page 63) is used to prevent a rippled edge on curved shirt hemlines.

Three Hems Using Serger with Conventional Machine

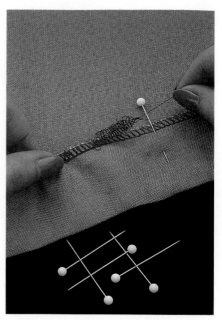

Overedged and blindstitched hem. Mark hem allowance, and grade seams in hem area. Serge hem edge. Fold hem as for blind hem, step 2, below. Pin hem into position, and blindstitch, using a conventional machine, or by hand.

Overedged and topstitched hem. Serge hem edge. Turn up hem; press. Topstitch from right side of garment, using conventional machine. Twin needle may be used for topstitching.

Eased hem. Ease hem fullness by pulling up needle thread. Or adjust differential feed, if available, to the ease setting. Pin hem into position; blindstitch, using a conventional machine, or by hand.

How to Overlock a Blind Hem

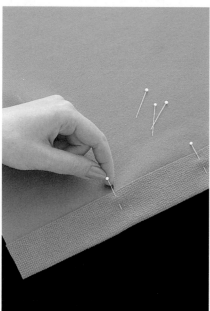

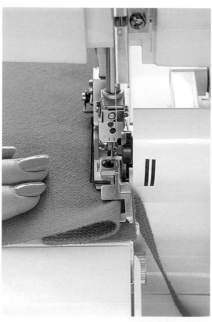

1) Adjust machine for flatlock stitch (page 74); use blind hem foot, if available. Set stitch length at 4 mm. Fold up hem; press. On hem side of garment, place pins with the heads toward body of garment.

2) Fold garment over hem allowance, with hem edge extending ¼" (6 mm) beyond fold. Stitch on extended hem edge, with needle *barely* catching fold; remove pins as you come to them.

3) Open hem, and pull fabric flat. Ladder of stitches shows on right side of lightweight fabrics, but is invisible on heavier textured fabrics.

How to Sew a Cover Stitch Hem

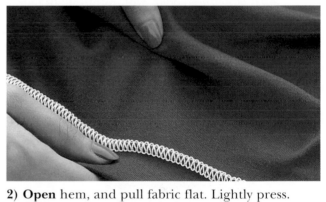

Split hem. Adjust machine for cover stitch (page 82). Press up hem. Place fabric under raised presser foot, right side up, with fold aligned to desired needle plate guide line. Holding threads, turn handwheel until needles enter fabric at beginning of hem. Stitch to fabric edge at end of hem; raise needles and presser foot. Holding stitches firmly, gently pull threads back. Cut threads, leaving tail; knot. Secure tails, using loop turner or needle (page 37).

Circular hem. Adjust machine and stitch hem as for split hem, left; start at back or side seam, and lap first stitches about 1" (2.5 cm). Raise needles and presser foot. Hold stitches behind foot firmly; gently pull fabric slightly back, and then to left. Cut thread tails. Pull out loose threads; secure threads, using fray check or knots as desired. Remove extra needle thread from surface of needle plate.

How to Flatlock a Sport Hem

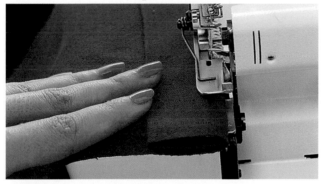

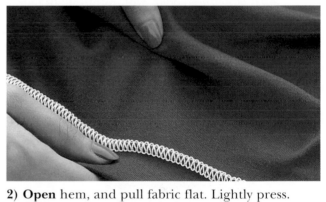

1) Adjust machine for flatlock stitch (pages 74 to 77). Fold up hem, and press. Fold up, and press again, enclosing raw edge; flatlock on fold (page 52), taking care to catch hem edge in stitches.

2) Open hem, and pull fabric flat. Lightly press. Decorative loops are on the right side of garment.

How to Flatlock a Fringed Hem

1) Mark placement line, by pulling a thread or using a marking pen, to indicate depth of fringe. Press a crease on marked line. Adjust serger for flatlock stitch (pages 74 to 77). Stitch on fold, as in steps 1 to 3, page 52.

2) Cut fabric up to stitches on grain every 3" (7.5 cm). Remove threads to create fringe. If flatlocking corners, apply liquid fray preventer to intersecting stitches, and use seam ripper to remove stitches in fringe area.

Rolled Hems

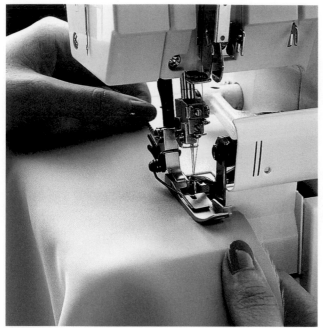

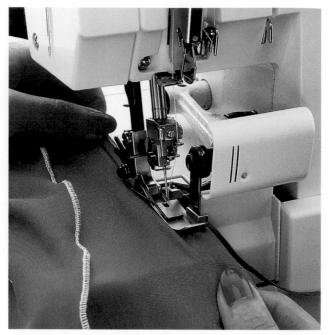

Rolled hem. Adjust machine for rolled hem stitch (pages 79 to 81). Hold tail chain at beginning of hem; stitch along hem edge, with right side of fabric facing up, trimming away hem allowance. Use taut sewing (page 106) or differential feed (page 46), if necessary, to prevent puckering.

Lettuce hem. Adjust machine for rolled hem stitch (pages 79 to 81). Stitch along hem edge, with right side of fabric facing up; stretch fabric taut, and trim edge slightly. Use differential feed (page 46), if desired.

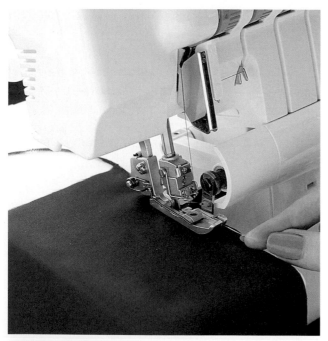

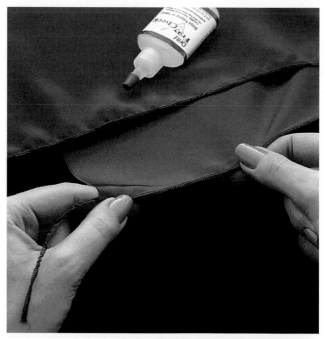

Fishline or wire hem. 1) Adjust machine for rolled hem stitch (pages 79 to 81). Test stitches for quality; some inserts may resist rolling. Insert fishline or wire through gimp foot (or under back and over front of regular presser foot). Run 4" (10 cm) tail. Stitch, trimming excess seam allowance; keep insert between needle and knives, if using regular presser foot.

2) Run 4" (10 cm) tail at end. Smooth out stitches; starting at center and working toward tails, ease puckered fabric over fishline or wire. Apply liquid fray preventer to end stitches; allow to dry. Trim tail chain close.

How to Prevent Ragged Edges on Rolled Hems

1) Test-sew rolled hem. Fabrics, such as loosely woven, metallic, or stiff fabrics, may not roll under, which causes a ragged edge.

2) Place a strip of tricot bias binding on upper side of fabric edge to be hemmed. Serge edge of fabric, catching binding in stitching.

3) Trim excess tricot bias binding close to rolled hem stitches, using sharp embroidery scissors.

Two Ways to Sew a Shirt-tail Hem

Serge hem edge; increase differential feed, if available, to ease curved edge slightly. Fold hem to wrong side of garment 1/8" (3 mm) beyond stitches; press. From right side, topstitch scant 1/4" (6 mm) from fold, using single or twin needle on conventional machine.

Serge to finish front and back edges of shirt before side seams are sewn; use differential feed, if available, to ease curves. Reset differential feed to normal. Press up hem 1/8" (3 mm) beyond stitches. Sew side seams, stitching through pressed hems. Secure tail chains (pages 36 and 37). Topstitch, using single or twin needle on conventional machine; pivot at side seams.

Adjusting the Stitches

Stitch width

Stitch length

Stitch Length & Width

It is important to check the stitch length and width for each fabric you sew by testing the stitches on a fabric scrap. The stitch length and width settings are comparable to the zigzag settings on the conventional machine. The same general principle of conventional sewing applies to serging; use shorter, narrower stitches for lightweight fabrics, and use longer, wider stitches for heavyweight fabrics. After changing stitch length or width on the serger, you may need to adjust the tensions, especially if the amount of change is significant.

Stitch Length

The stitch length is the distance in millimeters between the needle penetrations. The stitch length can be as short as 1 mm or as long as 5 mm. The stitch length is changed with a regulator dial or lever, depending on the model. Check the instruction manual for the location and the method of adjustment on your serger.

If the stitch length is too long, the stitches may pucker and the seams may not be strong enough to hold up under the stress of wearing the garment. A stitch length that is too short can weaken the seam in some fabrics, such as taffeta; the needle holes are too close together, and the needle perforates the fabric, causing the fabric to pull away from the stitches.

Fabric jams can occur if the stitch length is too short. Fabric does not feed properly through the machine, and stitches build up on the stitch finger. Correct a fabric jam as on page 45.

Stitch Width

The stitch width is the distance in millimeters between the needle thread and the trimmed edge of the fabric; if the serger has two needles, the stitch width is the distance from the left needle to the trimmed edge. The stitch width can be as narrow as 1.5 mm or as wide as 7.5 mm, depending on the model; some models have little or no variation in stitch width, which will limit the types of seams you can sew. On some 4/3-thread machines you can only adjust the stitch width by eliminating the left needle to sew a 3-thread overlock seam that is narrower.

Follow the instruction manual to change the stitch width. For some sergers, turn a dial to adjust the stitch width; for others, change the needle plate.

If the stitch width is too narrow, seams are not durable, and heavyweight fabrics do not press flat to one side. If the stitch width is too wide, stitches on lightweight fabrics may pucker.

Recommended Stitch Lengths and Widths

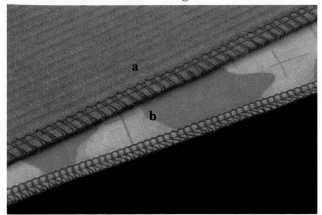

Stitch length. Use longer stitches (4 to 5 mm) on heavyweight fabrics (**a**); use shorter stitches (2 to 2.5 mm) on lightweight fabrics (**b**).

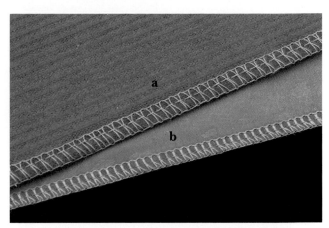

Stitch width. Use wider stitches (5 to 7.5 mm) for heavyweight fabrics (**a**); use narrower stitches (3.5 to 5 mm) for lightweight fabrics (**b**).

Stitch Length Problems

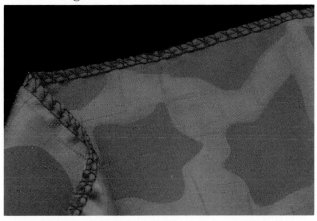

Stitch length too long. Seams on lightweight fabrics may pucker lengthwise, and stitches may show on right side of fabric.

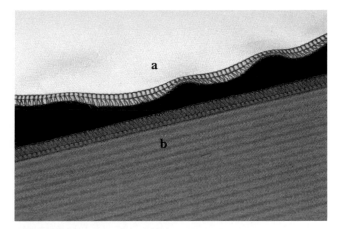

Stitch length too short. Seams may be weakened and perforated on fragile fabrics, and edges may stretch out of shape on outside curves (**a**). Seams may be too bulky on heavyweight fabrics (**b**), so fabric does not feed through serger easily.

Stitch Width Problems

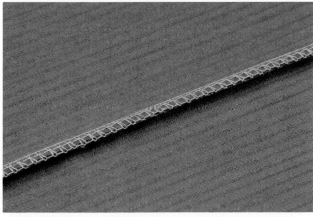

Stitch width too narrow. Seam may not be strong enough for heavyweight fabrics and may not press flat. On loosely woven fabrics, seam may ravel.

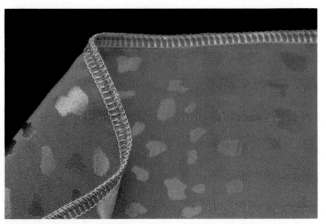

Stitch width too wide. Seams on lightweight fabrics may pucker under the stitches because wide stitches are too heavy for the fabric.

Adjusting Tension

Tension should be adjusted properly when sewing with a serger. If the stitch is not correct, check for proper threading before turning the tension dial. Even if only one thread has been snagged or has slipped out of a thread guide, it can appear that the tension needs adjusting. If a machine that has been sewing with correct tension has poor tension after the thread is changed, check the threading before adjusting tension dials.

When learning how to adjust the tension, thread the machine with colors of thread that match the color coding on the machine. This helps you to visualize and understand each thread path and how the threads interact with each other.

Practice Adjusting Thread Tensions

When the serger stitch has poor tension, only one thread may need adjustment. Adjust too tight threads first as they may cause other threads to seem loose even if they are not. Learning to adjust the correct thread or threads takes practice.

Sergers have the tensions preset at the factory for basic seaming. If the machine has numbered tension dials, write down preset numbers before practicing. Your instruction manual may also give recommended settings for all stitch types. Although factory and recommended settings will not give perfect tension for all fabrics, they do provide a good point of reference, especially for beginners.

Practice adjusting the tensions by sewing on a long strip of fabric. Start sewing, and slowly turn the tension dial for one of the threads to a lower number. As you sew, examine the stitches to see the change in the tension. The thread that has been adjusted will be slack or loose. Return the tension dial to the original setting.

Continue to sew, turning the same tension dial to a higher number. Examine the sample again to see how the tension has changed. The fabric puckers when one of the threads is too tight. Return the tension to the original setting. Continue to turn tension dials, one at a time, to see how each thread affects the stitch.

When looper tensions are correctly adjusted for a *balanced overedge stitch,* two opposing threads lock together at the edge of the fabric. When needle tensions are correctly adjusted, the threads rest smoothly on the top and are slightly visible on the underside. Looper threads, which intersect only the needle threads, form small, relaxed loops. Compare your stitches to the pictures on pages 70 to 83 if you are uncertain about which tension dial needs adjusting.

Tips for Analyzing Tension Problems

3-thread, 4-thread, and 5-thread overlock stitches

If fabric puckers lengthwise, one or both needle threads are too tight.

If fabric puckers crosswise under stitches, one or both looper threads are too tight.

If a looper thread can be moved easily or if it appears uneven, the looper thread is too loose.

If a needle thread forms loose loops on the underside of the fabric or if the seam pulls open, the needle thread is too loose.

If threads lock on upper side of fabric, either the upper looper threads are too tight, pulling to the upper side, or the lower looper threads are too loose, spilling over the edge.

If threads lock on underside of fabric, either the lower looper threads are too tight, pulling to the underside, or the upper looper threads are too loose, spilling over the edge.

2-thread chainstitch

If fabric puckers, one or both threads are too tight. Adjust each dial separately to determine which thread needs to be loosened.

If either thread can be moved easily or appears uneven, it is too loose.

2-thread overedge stitch

If fabric puckers, one or both threads are too tight.

If either thread can be moved easily or appears uneven, it is too loose.

If threads lock on upper side of fabric, either the looper thread is too tight, pulling to the upper side, or the needle thread is too loose, spilling over the edge.

If threads lock on underside of fabric, either the needle thread is too tight, pulling to the underside, or the looper thread is too loose, spilling over the edge.

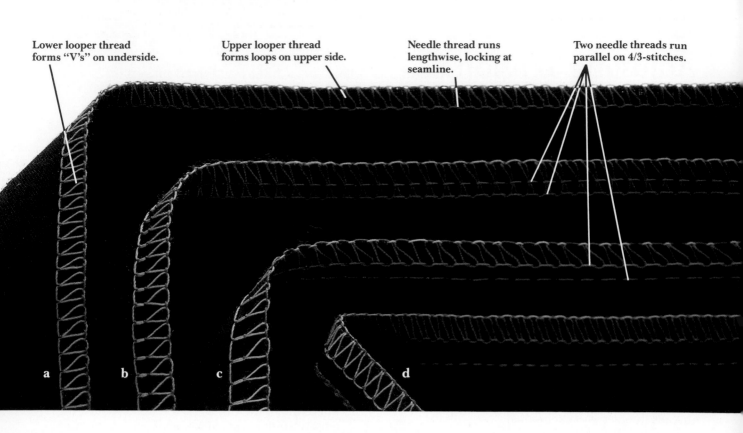

Lower looper thread forms "V's" on underside.

Upper looper thread forms loops on upper side.

Needle thread runs lengthwise, locking at seamline.

Two needle threads run parallel on 4/3-stitches.

a b c d

3-thread, 4-thread & 5-thread Overlock Stitches

The 3-thread overlock and the mock safety stitches are adjusted the same way. The overlock stitch (a) uses one needle to secure the stitches, and the mock safety stitches use two needles. There are two types of 4-thread mock safety stitches; on one, the upper looper thread locks at the left needle thread (b), and on the other, at the right needle thread (c), depending on the model. Both 3-thread overlock and 4-thread mock safety stitches are suitable for seaming wovens. Because these stitches stretch, they are also ideal for knits. The extra needle thread in the mock safety stitch makes it stronger than the overlock stitch.

On 5-thread sergers, the 5-thread safety stitch (d) is made up of a 3-thread overlock stitch and a 2-thread chainstitch. To adjust the chainstitch, refer to page 72. Use the 5-thread safety stitch for sewing woven fabrics or stable knits.

Tension Adjustments (3-thread overlock and 4-thread mock safety)

Upper looper thread too tight.
Upper looper thread (orange) pulls lower looper thread (yellow) to upper side of fabric, causing fabric to pucker or curl under stitches. Loosen upper looper thread tension dial until looper threads lock at edge.

Upper looper thread too loose.
Upper looper thread (orange) spills over cut edge to underside of fabric. Upper looper threads are slack and can be moved easily. Fabric does not pucker or curl under stitches. Tighten upper looper thread tension dial until looper threads lock at edge.

Lower looper thread too tight.
Lower looper thread (yellow) pulls upper looper thread (orange) to underside of fabric, causing fabric to pucker or curl under stitches. Loosen lower looper thread tension dial until looper threads lock at edge.

Lower looper thread too loose.
Lower looper thread (yellow) spills over cut edge to upper side of fabric. Lower looper threads are slack and can be moved easily. Fabric does not pucker or curl under stitches. Tighten lower looper thread tension dial until looper threads lock at edge.

Both looper threads too tight.
Looper threads (orange and yellow) may lock at edge, but fabric is puckered or bunched under stitches. Stitches are narrower than stitch width setting on serger. Loosen both looper thread tension dials until fabric is smooth under stitches.

Both looper threads too loose. Both looper threads (orange and yellow) extend over cut edge in loose loops. Tighten both looper thread tension dials until threads hug edge.

Needle threads too tight. Fabric puckers lengthwise. Loosen one or both needle thread (blue and green) tension dials until fabric lies smooth without puckers. Test stitches in knit fabrics by stretching; loosen needle thread tension dials, if necessary.

Needle threads too loose. Needle threads (blue and green) form loose loops on underside of fabric (a). Seam pulls open on right side, exposing stitches (b). Tighten one or both needle thread tension dials until seam closes without puckers.

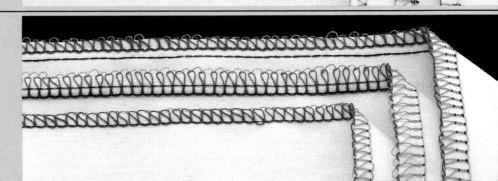

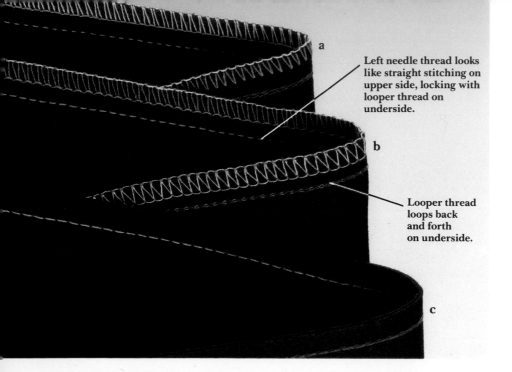

Left needle thread looks like straight stitching on upper side, locking with looper thread on underside.

a

b

Looper thread loops back and forth on underside.

c

The 4-thread safety stitch (**a**) sewn on a 4/2-thread serger is really two rows of stitches, stitched at the same time: the 2-thread chainstitch or *safety stitch,* below, and the 2-thread overedge, opposite.

The 5-thread safety stitch (**b**) sewn on a 5-thread serger consists of two rows of stitches: the 2-thread chainstitch, and the 3-thread overlock stitch, pages 69 to 71.

The chainstitch (**c**) may be used alone for decorative topstitching, or for basting. Always disengage the upper knife in these cases; follow the directions in your instruction manual.

Tension Adjustments (chainstitches)

Lower looper thread too tight. Lower looper thread (purple) is tight and drawn on underside of fabric, causing puckered seam and skipped stitches. Loosen lower looper thread tension dial until even loops are formed. If problem is not solved, check for tight needle thread tension.

Lower looper thread too loose. Large, loose loops form in lower looper thread (purple), causing seam to pull open, exposing stitches on right side of fabric. Tighten lower looper thread tension dial until even loops form on underside.

Left needle thread too tight. Tight left needle thread (blue) may cause puckered seam and skipped stitches. Loosen left needle thread tension dial until fabric does not pucker. If problem is not solved, check for tight lower looper thread tension.

Left needle thread too loose. Left needle thread (blue) forms large loops on underside of fabric. Seam may pull open, exposing stitches on right side of fabric. Tighten left needle thread tension dial until close, firm loops form on underside.

2-thread Overedge Stitches

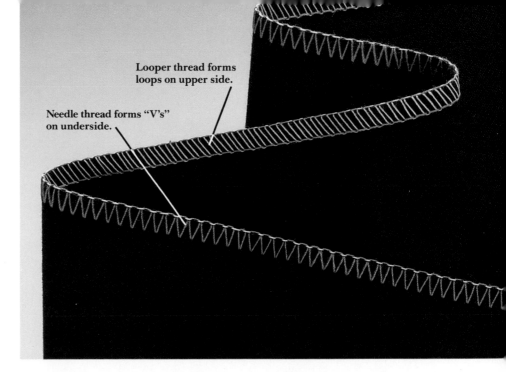

Looper thread forms loops on upper side.

Needle thread forms "V's" on underside.

The 2-thread overedge stitch is formed with one needle and one looper; depending on the model, either the upper or lower looper is used. Consult the instruction manual for specific instructions on the 2-thread stitch. Then adjust the tensions as shown, below.

The 2-thread overedge stitch is used as a lightweight seam finish. Because less thread is used for the stitches, they do not imprint on the right side of the fabric when pressed.

Tension Adjustments (2-thread overedge stitch)

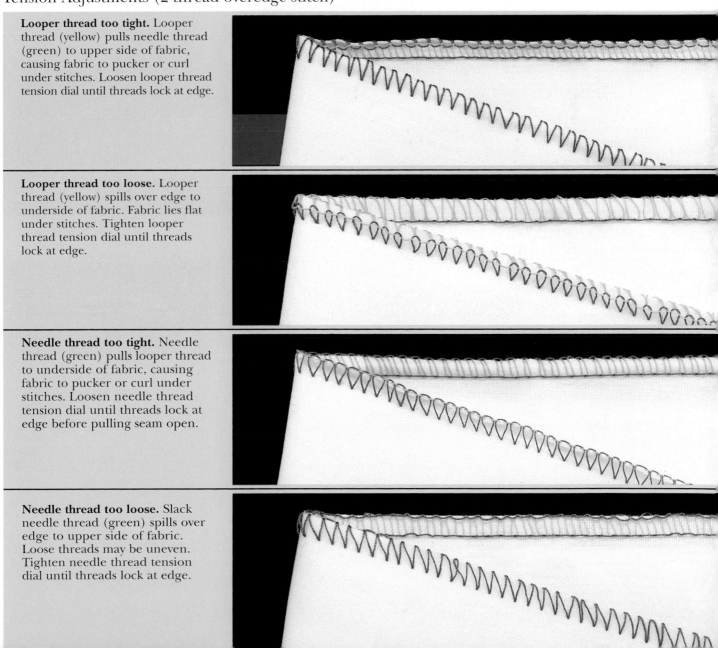

Looper thread too tight. Looper thread (yellow) pulls needle thread (green) to upper side of fabric, causing fabric to pucker or curl under stitches. Loosen looper thread tension dial until threads lock at edge.

Looper thread too loose. Looper thread (yellow) spills over edge to underside of fabric. Fabric lies flat under stitches. Tighten looper thread tension dial until threads lock at edge.

Needle thread too tight. Needle thread (green) pulls looper thread to underside of fabric, causing fabric to pucker or curl under stitches. Loosen needle thread tension dial until threads lock at edge before pulling seam open.

Needle thread too loose. Slack needle thread (green) spills over edge to upper side of fabric. Loose threads may be uneven. Tighten needle thread tension dial until threads lock at edge.

Flatlock Stitches

Flatlock stitching can be used decoratively for the look of applied trim on a garment. It may also be used to serge nonbulky seams on tricot. Decorative threads may be used in the serger for special effects; to learn how to serge with decorative threads, see pages 114 to 119.

Most models or brands of sergers are capable of creating flatlock stitches; however, the tension range of some sergers may be too limited to sew perfect flatlock stitches. Flatlock stitches are sewn with either two or three threads, depending on the model; some have the option of both 2-thread and 3-thread flatlocking. Refer to the instruction manual for specific directions for each model.

The 3-thread flatlock stitch is sewn with one needle, and upper and lower loopers. The 2-thread flatlock stitch is sewn with one needle and one looper; depending on the model, either the upper or lower looper is used.

To flatlock, first adjust the tension setting, as described on pages 75 to 77. The seam is then stitched and pulled apart to flatten the fabric layers at the seamline. Test the tension setting before pulling the fabric flat; it is easier to identify a stitch problem before fabric is pulled. If tension is not adjusted correctly, fabric will not pull flat.

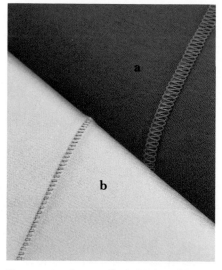

Decorative loop effect (**a**) is achieved when flatlock seam is stitched wrong sides together. For ladder effect (**b**), stitch seam right sides together.

Basic Tension Adjustments for Flatlock Stitches

2-thread flatlock stitch

Adjust stitch length as desired before adjusting tension.

Start with a 3-thread balanced stitch (pages 69 to 71) before adjusting tension for 2-thread flatlock; or use 2-thread overedge stitch (pages 69 and 73), which does not require further tension adjustments.

Loosen needle tension dial generously so needle thread extends to the edge of fabric on underside.

Loosen looper tension dial slightly, if necessary, to allow fabric to pull open flat.

3-thread flatlock stitch

Adjust stitch length as desired before adjusting tension.

Start with a 3-thread balanced stitch (pages 69 to 71) before adjusting tension for 3-thread flatlock.

Loosen needle tension dial generously so needle thread extends to the edge of fabric on underside.

Tighten lower looper tension dial generously so lower looper thread pulls into a straight line at edge of fabric.

Loosen upper looper thread slightly, if necessary, to allow fabric to pull open flat.

How to Flatlock a Seam (knit fabric)

1) Adjust tension for flatlock stitch. Serge the seam, trimming excess seam allowance.

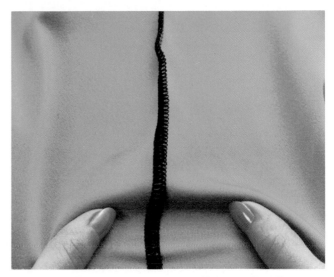

2) Pull crosswise on the seam, pulling stitches flat.

How to Flatlock a Seam (woven fabric)

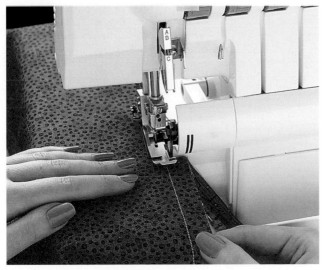

1) Stitch seam, wrong sides together, using conventional machine. Adjust tension for flatlock stitch. Serge over seam, aligning straight stitches to center of serged stitches.

2) Pull fabric flat, as in step 2, above. Press seam; press lightly on wrong side, if using decorative threads.

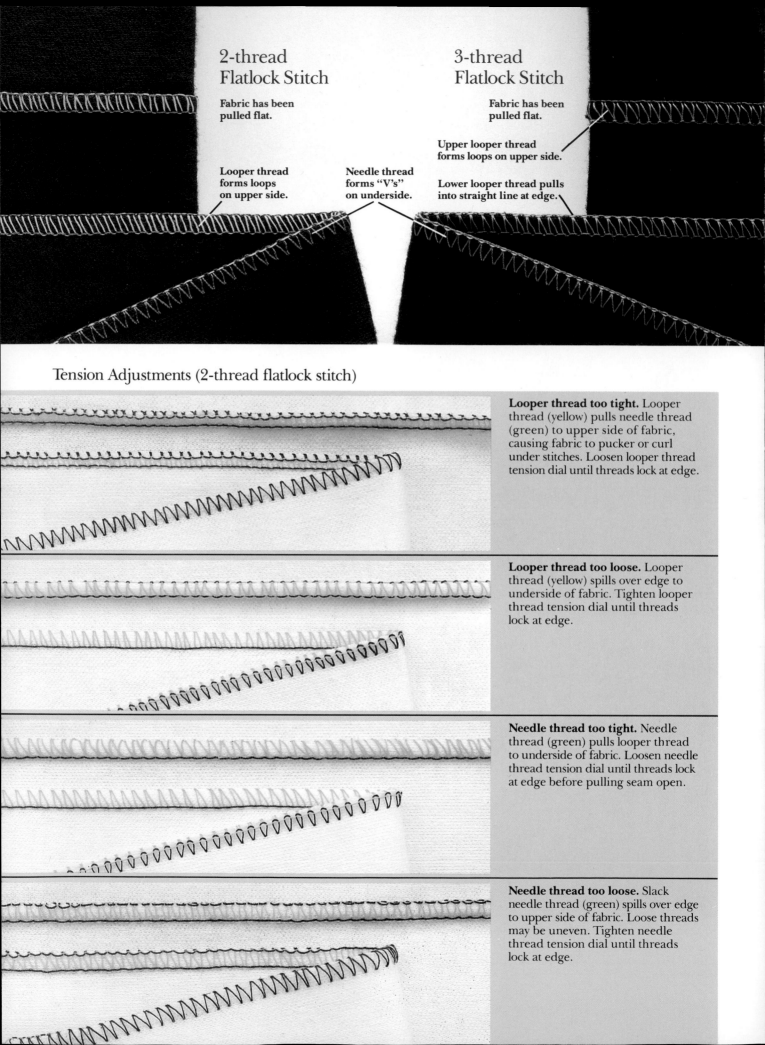

2-thread Flatlock Stitch

Fabric has been pulled flat.

Looper thread forms loops on upper side.

Needle thread forms "V's" on underside.

3-thread Flatlock Stitch

Fabric has been pulled flat.

Upper looper thread forms loops on upper side.

Lower looper thread pulls into straight line at edge.

Tension Adjustments (2-thread flatlock stitch)

Looper thread too tight. Looper thread (yellow) pulls needle thread (green) to upper side of fabric, causing fabric to pucker or curl under stitches. Loosen looper thread tension dial until threads lock at edge.

Looper thread too loose. Looper thread (yellow) spills over edge to underside of fabric. Tighten looper thread tension dial until threads lock at edge.

Needle thread too tight. Needle thread (green) pulls looper thread to underside of fabric. Loosen needle thread tension dial until threads lock at edge before pulling seam open.

Needle thread too loose. Slack needle thread (green) spills over edge to upper side of fabric. Loose threads may be uneven. Tighten needle thread tension dial until threads lock at edge.

Tension Adjustments (3-thread flatlock stitch)

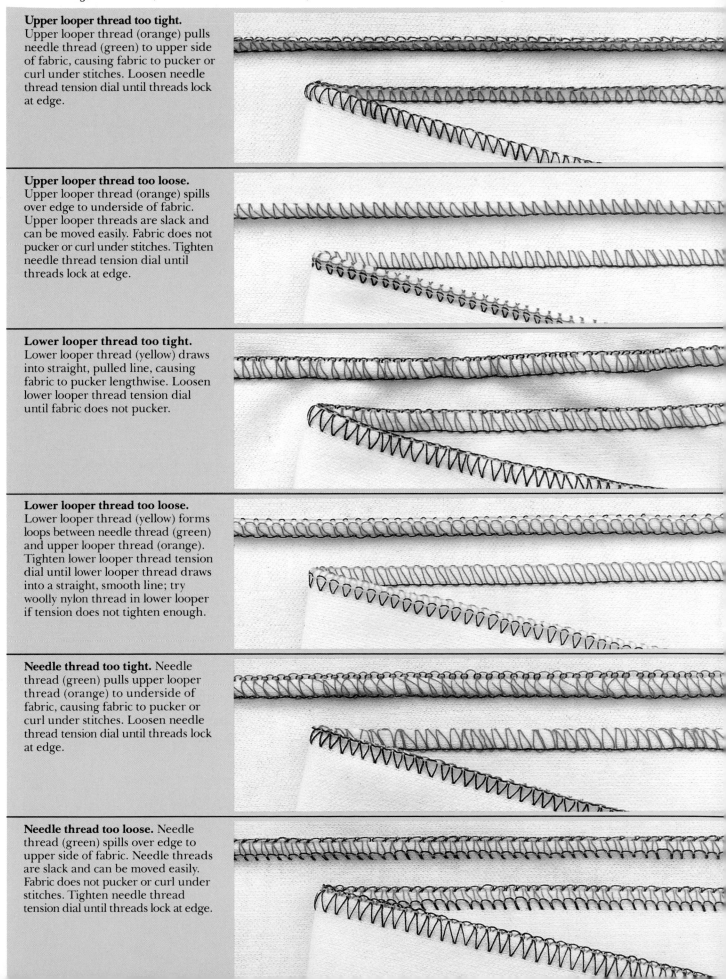

Upper looper thread too tight.
Upper looper thread (orange) pulls needle thread (green) to upper side of fabric, causing fabric to pucker or curl under stitches. Loosen needle thread tension dial until threads lock at edge.

Upper looper thread too loose.
Upper looper thread (orange) spills over edge to underside of fabric. Upper looper threads are slack and can be moved easily. Fabric does not pucker or curl under stitches. Tighten needle thread tension dial until threads lock at edge.

Lower looper thread too tight.
Lower looper thread (yellow) draws into straight, pulled line, causing fabric to pucker lengthwise. Loosen lower looper thread tension dial until fabric does not pucker.

Lower looper thread too loose.
Lower looper thread (yellow) forms loops between needle thread (green) and upper looper thread (orange). Tighten lower looper thread tension dial until lower looper draws into a straight, smooth line; try woolly nylon thread in lower looper if tension does not tighten enough.

Needle thread too tight. Needle thread (green) pulls upper looper thread (orange) to underside of fabric, causing fabric to pucker or curl under stitches. Loosen needle thread tension dial until threads lock at edge.

Needle thread too loose. Needle thread (green) spills over edge to upper side of fabric. Needle threads are slack and can be moved easily. Fabric does not pucker or curl under stitches. Tighten needle thread tension dial until threads lock at edge.

Rolled Hem Stitches

Most sergers can make a rolled hem stitch. Some models require additional accessories, such as a different needle plate, presser foot, or auxiliary tension dial; others have a built-in rolled hem feature.

The rolled hem stitch is sewn using either two or three threads, depending on the serger model; on some models you may sew both 2-thread and 3-thread rolled hems. Refer to the instruction manual for specific directions for each machine.

A 3-thread rolled hem is suitable for most lightweight to mediumweight fabrics. A 2-thread rolled hem is preferred for fine, lightweight edge finishes on sheers and lightweight fabrics.

The stitch length adjustment is critical to the finished look of the rolled hem stitch. If the stitch length is too short, the stitching may fall off the edge or it may be too heavy for lightweight fabrics, causing a stiffer edge; if too long, the fabric may pucker. Before sewing your project, practice stitching on fabric scraps. To achieve perfect rolled hem stitches, refer to the information below and on pages 80 and 81. You may choose to use tricot bias binding to stabilize a lace edge; lay a narrow strip of binding on top of the lace, as shown on page 63. You may choose to try a bulky thread like texturized nylon to visually fill in a longer stitch length; see pages 114 to 121 for working with decorative threads.

Basic Tension Adjustments for Rolled Hem Stitches

2-thread rolled hem stitch	3-thread rolled hem stitch
Adjust stitch length to 1.5 or 2 mm setting for a soft edge finish.	**Adjust** stitch length to under 1 mm for a filled-in edge finish that has body or stiffness; adjust stitch length to 2 mm for a softer edge finish that is less filled-in.
Start with a balanced 3-thread overlock stitch (pages 69 to 71) or a 2-thread overedge stitch (pages 69 and 73) before adjusting tension for 2-thread rolled hem. Tension adjustments may be unnecessary or slight if starting with a balanced 3-thread overlock stitch.	**Start** with a balanced overlock stitch (pages 69 to 71) before adjusting tension for 3-thread rolled hem.
Tighten needle thread tension dial to eliminate "V's" formed by needle thread on underside of fabric.	**Tighten** lower looper thread tension dial so upper looper thread is pulled around the edge of the fabric to the underside for a rounded rolled hem.
Loosen looper thread tension dial so looper thread rolls around edge to upper side of fabric.	**Loosen** upper looper thread tension dial in addition to tightening lower looper thread tension dial for a flat, less-rounded, rolled hem.
	Loosen needle thread tension dial slightly if fabric puckers lengthwise, or stitch using taut sewing (page 106).

How to Sew a Rolled Hem

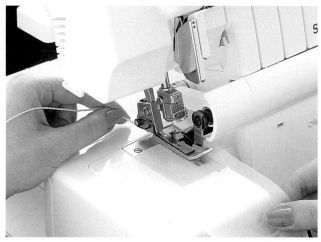

1) Adjust machine for rolled hem stitch, above and on pages 80 and 81. Hold tail chain at beginning of hem to keep it from curling into looper area.

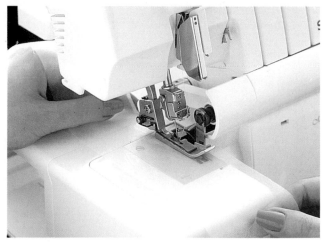

2) Stitch along hem edge, with right side of fabric facing up; trim away hem allowance. Use taut sewing (page 106) or differential feed (page 46), if necessary, to prevent puckering.

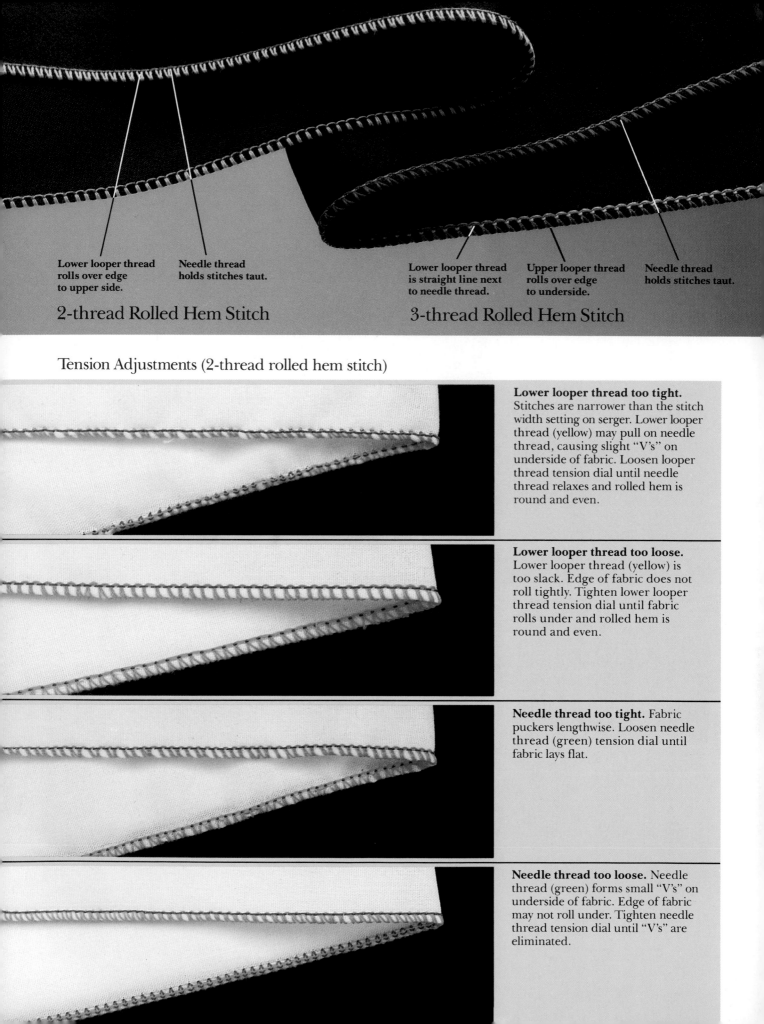

Lower looper thread rolls over edge to upper side.

Needle thread holds stitches taut.

2-thread Rolled Hem Stitch

Lower looper thread is straight line next to needle thread.

Upper looper thread rolls over edge to underside.

Needle thread holds stitches taut.

3-thread Rolled Hem Stitch

Tension Adjustments (2-thread rolled hem stitch)

Lower looper thread too tight. Stitches are narrower than the stitch width setting on serger. Lower looper thread (yellow) may pull on needle thread, causing slight "V's" on underside of fabric. Loosen looper thread tension dial until needle thread relaxes and rolled hem is round and even.

Lower looper thread too loose. Lower looper thread (yellow) is too slack. Edge of fabric does not roll tightly. Tighten lower looper thread tension dial until fabric rolls under and rolled hem is round and even.

Needle thread too tight. Fabric puckers lengthwise. Loosen needle thread (green) tension dial until fabric lays flat.

Needle thread too loose. Needle thread (green) forms small "V's" on underside of fabric. Edge of fabric may not roll under. Tighten needle thread tension dial until "V's" are eliminated.

Tension Adjustments (3-thread rolled hem stitch)

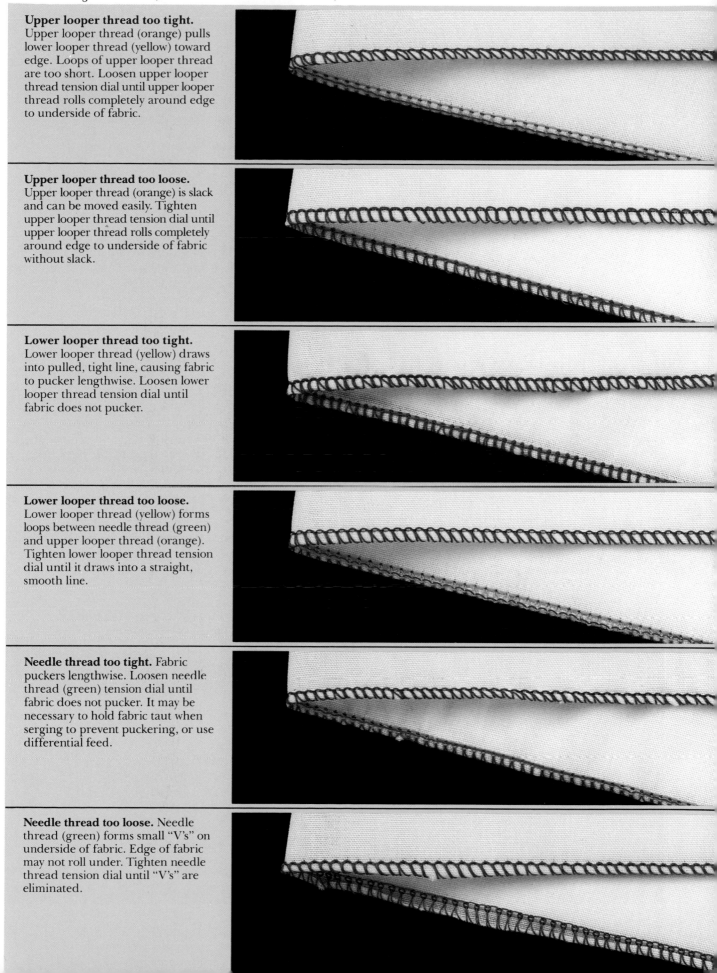

Upper looper thread too tight. Upper looper thread (orange) pulls lower looper thread (yellow) toward edge. Loops of upper looper thread are too short. Loosen upper looper thread tension dial until upper looper thread rolls completely around edge to underside of fabric.

Upper looper thread too loose. Upper looper thread (orange) is slack and can be moved easily. Tighten upper looper thread tension dial until upper looper thread rolls completely around edge to underside of fabric without slack.

Lower looper thread too tight. Lower looper thread (yellow) draws into pulled, tight line, causing fabric to pucker lengthwise. Loosen lower looper thread tension dial until fabric does not pucker.

Lower looper thread too loose. Lower looper thread (yellow) forms loops between needle thread (green) and upper looper thread (orange). Tighten lower looper thread tension dial until it draws into a straight, smooth line.

Needle thread too tight. Fabric puckers lengthwise. Loosen needle thread (green) tension dial until fabric does not pucker. It may be necessary to hold fabric taut when serging to prevent puckering, or use differential feed.

Needle thread too loose. Needle thread (green) forms small "V's" on underside of fabric. Edge of fabric may not roll under. Tighten needle thread tension dial until "V's" are eliminated.

Cover Stitch

In the cover stitch, a single looper thread secures parallel rows of linear surface stitches. Familiar as a common ready-to-wear stitch, it was once available only on industrial sergers. Today, some 5-thread sergers can be converted to sew a 3-thread cover stitch. The upper knife is disengaged, and specialized throat plates and presser feet are attached; refer to the machine manual for specific directions.

The cover stitch may be used to seam fabrics, but it is most often used to topstitch or bind hems and necklines. Because it has considerable stretch, it is popular for attaching elastic and hemming low-stretch to high-stretch knits. Since the fabric can be positioned so the looper thread encloses the cut edge, it is also suitable for lightweight to mediumweight wovens.

Looper thread connects, both within and between, the parallel rows of straight stitches on the underside. Needle threads look like straight stitching on upper side, locking with looper thread on underside.

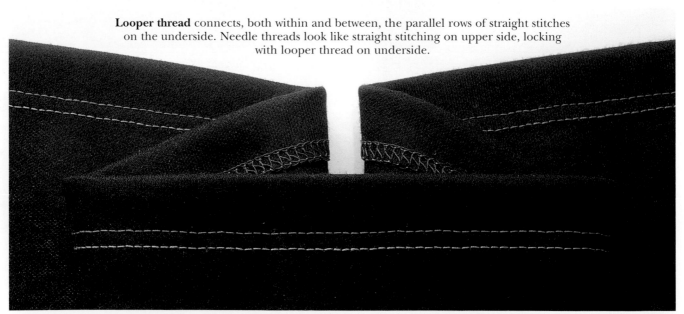

Tension Adjustments (cover stitch)

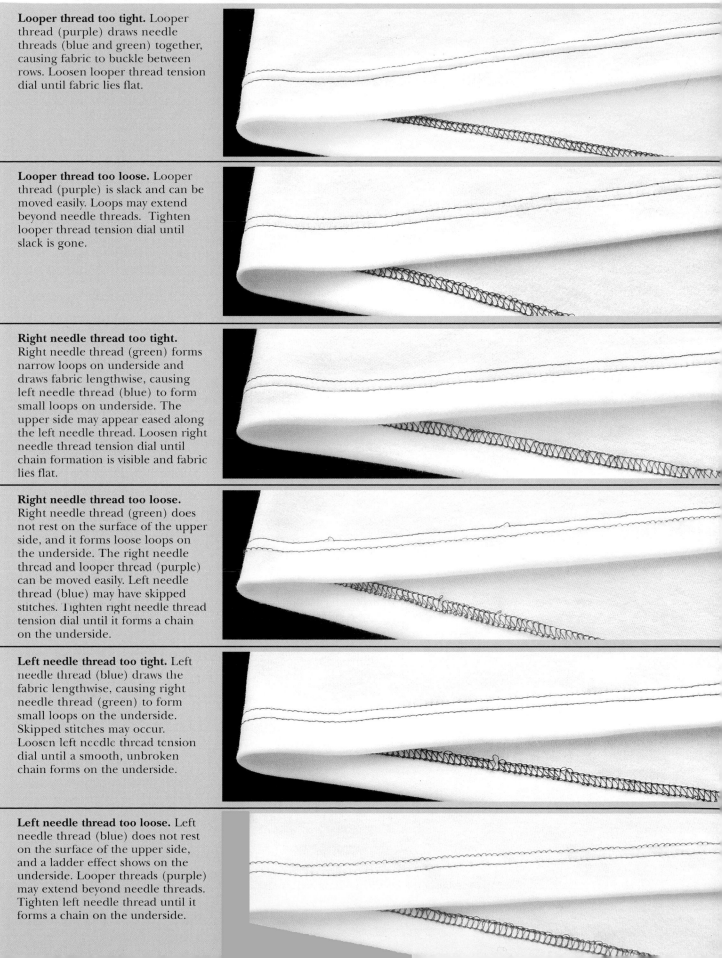

Looper thread too tight. Looper thread (purple) draws needle threads (blue and green) together, causing fabric to buckle between rows. Loosen looper thread tension dial until fabric lies flat.

Looper thread too loose. Looper thread (purple) is slack and can be moved easily. Loops may extend beyond needle threads. Tighten looper thread tension dial until slack is gone.

Right needle thread too tight. Right needle thread (green) forms narrow loops on underside and draws fabric lengthwise, causing left needle thread (blue) to form small loops on underside. The upper side may appear eased along the left needle thread. Loosen right needle thread tension dial until chain formation is visible and fabric lies flat.

Right needle thread too loose. Right needle thread (green) does not rest on the surface of the upper side, and it forms loose loops on the underside. The right needle thread and looper thread (purple) can be moved easily. Left needle thread (blue) may have skipped stitches. Tighten right needle thread tension dial until it forms a chain on the underside.

Left needle thread too tight. Left needle thread (blue) draws the fabric lengthwise, causing right needle thread (green) to form small loops on the underside. Skipped stitches may occur. Loosen left needle thread tension dial until a smooth, unbroken chain forms on the underside.

Left needle thread too loose. Left needle thread (blue) does not rest on the surface of the upper side, and a ladder effect shows on the underside. Looper threads (purple) may extend beyond needle threads. Tighten left needle thread until it forms a chain on the underside.

Garment Construction

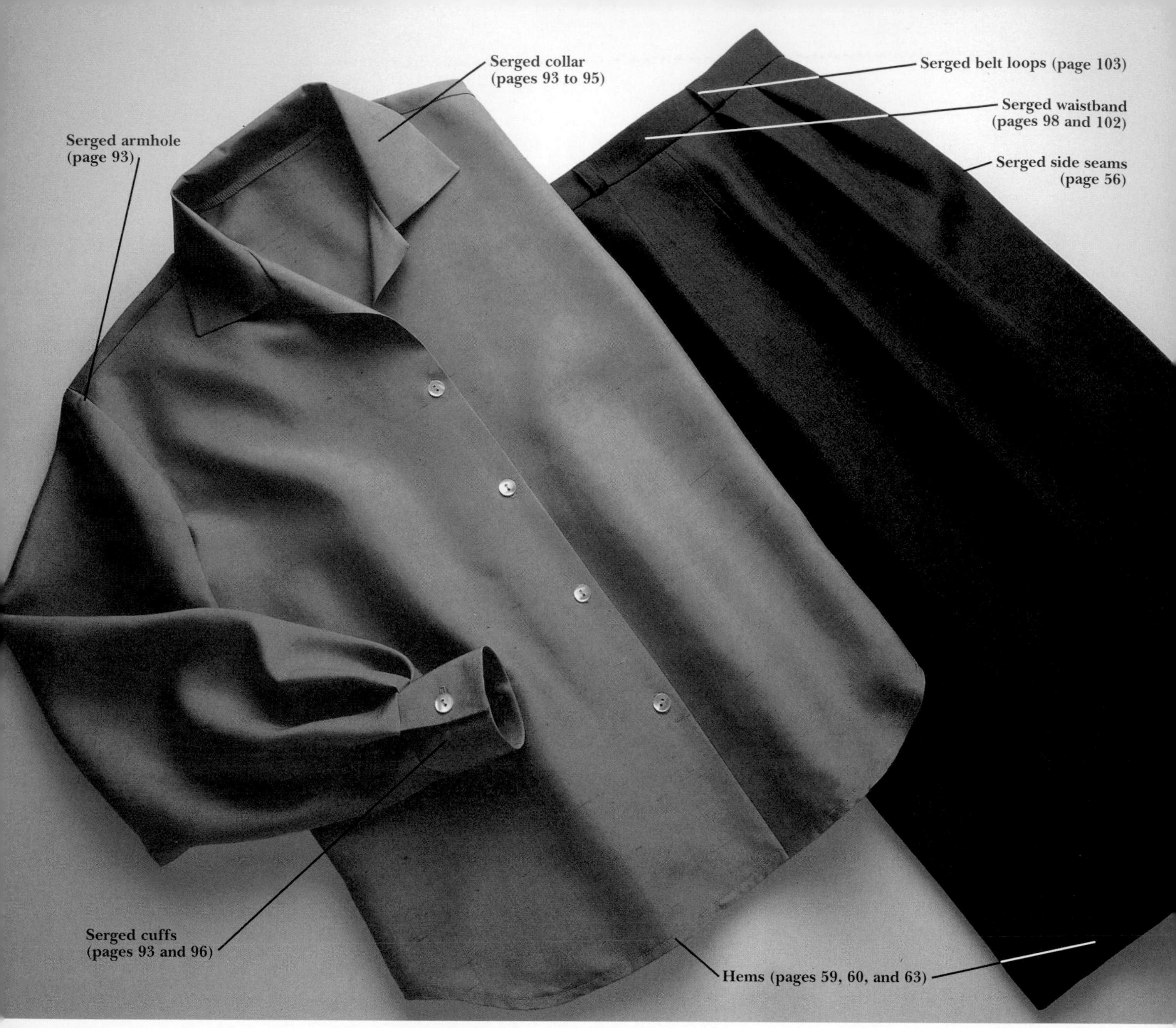

Serged armhole
(page 93)

Serged collar
(pages 93 to 95)

Serged belt loops (page 103)

Serged waistband
(pages 98 and 102)

Serged side seams
(page 56)

Serged cuffs
(pages 93 and 96)

Hems (pages 59, 60, and 63)

Garment Construction

Special methods have been developed for sewing many garment details on a serger. Depending on the style or the fabric, some garments may be sewn entirely on a serger; others may also require the use of a conventional machine.

The direction sheets of many current patterns include instructions for using the serger. This section examines which garment details can be serged and which should be sewn conventionally; you may discover

additional areas where you can use the serger for efficiency or personal design details.

Garments requiring critical fitting adjustments are usually sewn on the conventional machine to allow room for adjustment in the seam allowances. When overlocked seams are used, baste (page 54) or pin-fit the garment before sewing the seams.

Serged stitches must not be clipped, or they will ravel. Curves or corners that require clipping, such

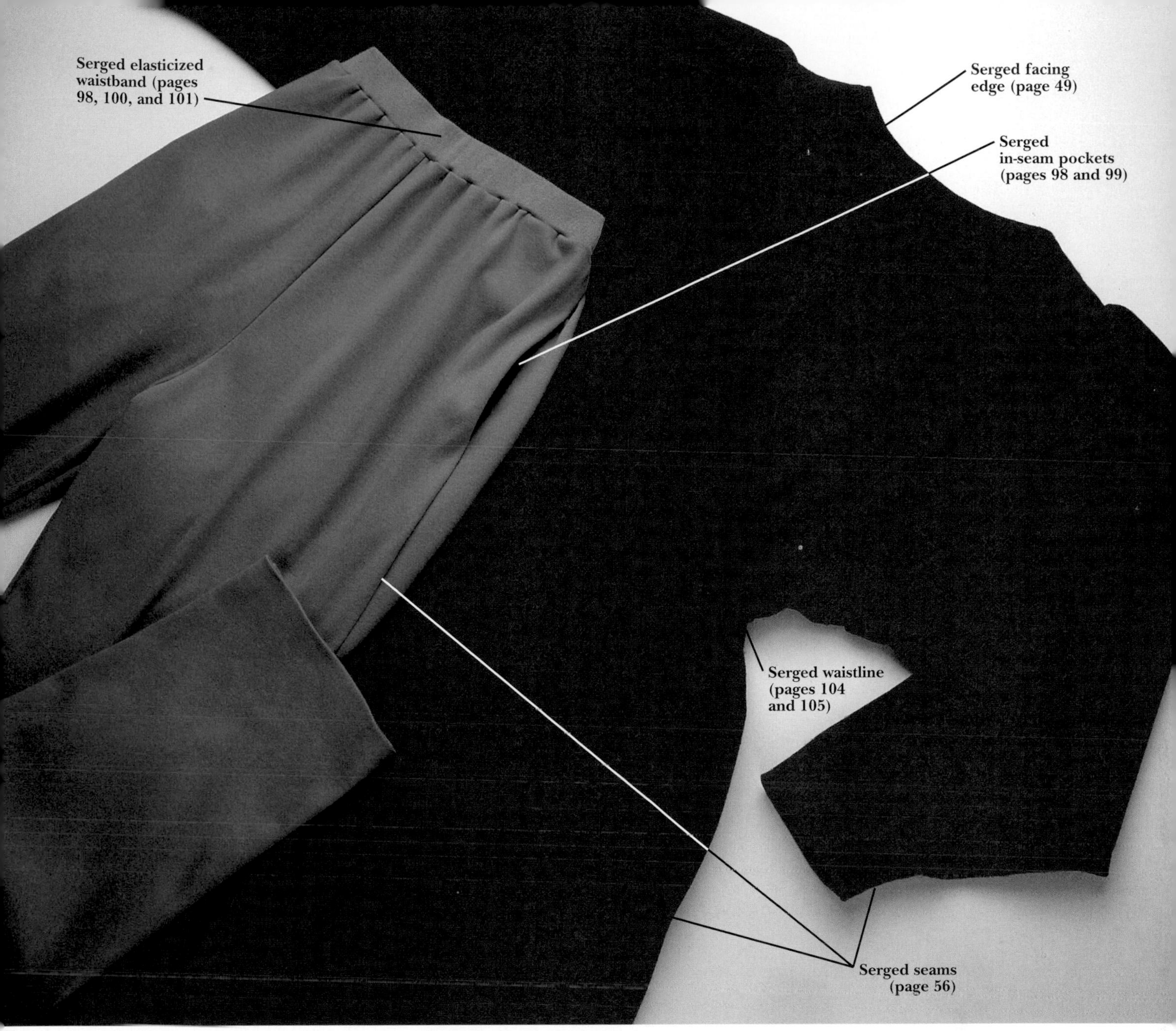

Serged elasticized
waistband (pages
98, 100, and 101)

Serged facing
edge (page 49)

Serged
in-seam pockets
(pages 98 and 99)

Serged waistline
(pages 104
and 105)

Serged seams
(page 56)

as enclosed neckline seams, are sewn using the conventional machine. Seams with a side or back slit are also sewn using the conventional machine because the seam allowances must be pressed open to form the slit facing.

The serger's elongated presser foot can make it difficult to stitch details precisely. Areas where precise stitch placement is required, such as jacket lapels, should be sewn using the conventional machine. To ensure accuracy and smooth fit, darts should also be

sewn on the conventional machine. Zippers are applied and buttonholes are sewn on the conventional machine, using specialized presser feet.

When the serger's upper knife is disengaged, the chainstitch is appropriate for topstitching. Because the stitch looks different on the upper and underside of the fabric, the conventional machine is used whenever straight stitches are desired on both sides of the garment.

Pullover Tops

A pullover top finished with ribbing is an ideal first project. The basic design can be varied in many ways, including fabric choices from basic knits to a silky woven or challis. A dress or shell can be made from the same basic design, simply by changing the finished length.

A cotton interlock knit is the easiest fabric to use for the front, back, and sleeve pieces. Ribbing for the neck edge, cuffs, and lower band is available in several weights as well as a range of coordinating or contrasting colors.

Pullover patterns are usually designed with 5/8" (1.5 cm) or 1/4" (6 mm) seams. Since the serger automatically trims away excess seam allowances as it stitches, patterns with either seam allowance width may be used. A pattern with a loose fit and a neckline seam measurement equal to or greater than the head measurement is necessary if using a woven fabric.

There are two methods for serging a pullover top or T-shirt. The flat construction method is faster; however, the seams may be noticeable at the ribbing edges. The in-the-round method encloses the ribbing seams for a neater, better-quality finish. You may want to try both methods to decide which one you prefer.

How to Sew a Pullover Top (flat method)

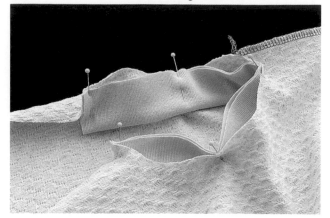

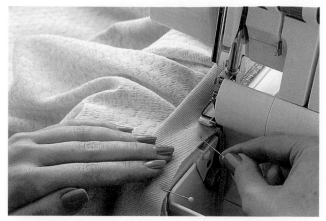

1) Stitch one shoulder seam. Fold neck ribbing in half lengthwise. Divide neck edge and ribbing into fourths; pin-mark. Pin ribbing to neckline, right sides together, matching pins.

2) Set differential feed to a larger number, if differential feed is available. Stitch ribbing to neckline, stretching ribbing to fit; remove pins just before they reach the knives.

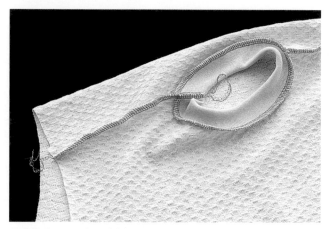

3) Apply cuff ribbings to sleeves, as for neckline ribbing, steps 1 and 2, above. Reset differential feed to normal, if necessary.

4) Pin-baste shoulder seam, matching neckline seams; turn seam allowances in opposite directions to minimize bulk, if desired. Overlock seam, stitching toward neck. Secure tail chains (pages 36 and 37).

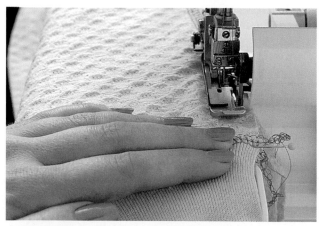

5) Stitch sleeves into armholes. Pin-baste side seams, matching underarm seams, cuff seams, and cuff folds. Overlock one side and sleeve seam from lower edge of garment to cuff folds; remove pins as you come to them.

6) Apply lower edge band, as for neckline ribbing, steps 1 and 2, above. Reset differential feed to normal, if necessary. Pin-baste and stitch remaining side and sleeve seam. Secure tail chains at lower band and cuff edges.

How to Sew a Pullover Top (in-the-round method)

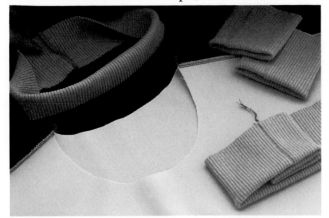

1) Stitch both shoulder seams. Sew ends of each ribbing piece, using an overlock or conventional machine. Fold overlocked seams in opposite directions at seamline, or press conventional seams open. Fold ribbing pieces in half lengthwise, wrong sides together.

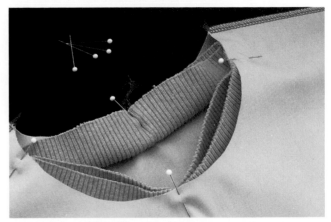

2) Divide neckline edge and ribbing into fourths; pin-mark. Pin ribbing to neckline, right sides together, matching markings. Place ribbing seam in center back.

3) Stitch ribbing to neckline as in step 2, opposite. Reset differential feed to normal, if necessary. Press seam allowances at neckline toward body of garment. Edgestitch, if desired, using conventional machine.

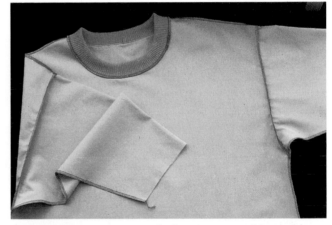

4) Stitch sleeves into armholes. Sew one side and sleeve seam, from lower edge of garment to lower edge of sleeve, matching underarm seam. Repeat for other side and sleeve seam.

5) Pin-mark sleeve edge and cuff ribbing into fourths. Pin cuff to sleeve, right sides together, matching seams. Adjust differential feed, if available. Overlock, stretching cuff to fit and removing pins.

6) Pin-mark lower garment edge and band ribbing into fourths. Pin band to garment, right sides together, matching band seam to a side seam. Overlock, stretching band to fit. Reset differential feed to normal.

Blouses

There are many timesaving methods for sewing blouses and shirts, even those with a convertible collar and set-in sleeves with cuffs.

Overlock seaming offers advantages beyond speedy construction. The seams in soft or silky fabrics are less likely to pucker when sewn on a serger. On semi-sheers, the narrow seams are less conspicuous than pressed-open conventional seams. Serged seams also require less pressing to remain neat and flat after laundering.

As with any project, always test the stitch on scraps of the fabric before beginning to sew the garment itself. Adjust the stitch width and length, and the thread tensions, until the seam is balanced and pucker-free. If you are in doubt about whether the garment will fit correctly, baste the main garment pieces before serging the seams (page 54).

A serger may be used almost entirely for the construction of a traditional blouse that has a convertible collar and set-in cuffed sleeves. Use a conventional machine for sewing areas with points to turn and for sewing on buttons and making buttonholes.

Collars

Sergers may be used to stitch collar seams with gradual curves. This is especially helpful to prevent show-through of clipped and graded seam allowances on lightweight or sheer fabrics. Use a 3-thread overlock stitch for lightweight, flexible stitches and minimal bulk.

Exposed collar seams may be stitched on the serger for a decorative effect. Use the rolled hem stitch and high-quality thread for beautiful stitches. A heavier thread, such as buttonhole twist, pearl cotton, or texturized nylon, can be used to create a piping effect on collars that are made from mediumweight fabrics.

Use a conventional machine to stitch collars that require grading and clipping. A conventional machine is always used to stitch enclosed seams on collars with points.

Interface collars and facings according to the fabric and pattern selected. Neck facings may be eliminated when applying collars with a serger. For convertible collars, eliminate the back neck facing only. If facings are desired, finish the edges of the facings with a 2-thread overedge or 3-thread overlock stitch. A faced neckline seam may be serged unless it requires trimming and clipping, as would a square or V neckline.

Cuffs, Plackets & Sleeves

A slashed placket sleeve opening may be serged, which is faster and easier than sewing a continuous lap placket. This method may be used for a cuff with or without an underlap extension.

If your cuff pattern piece does not have an underlap extension, the slash opening may be eliminated; the lower edge of the sleeve is stitched to the cuff in one quick step.

Raglan or dropped-shoulder sleeve seams can be stitched on the serger. Standard set-in sleeves should be set in according to the pattern instructions, using the conventional machine. Overedge the armhole seam through both layers, 1/8" (3 mm) away from the conventional stitches, to finish the seams. The conventional machine gives you better control when stitching the eased sleeve seam. The extra row of stitching adds strength, which is especially desirable in fitted garments that have set-in sleeves.

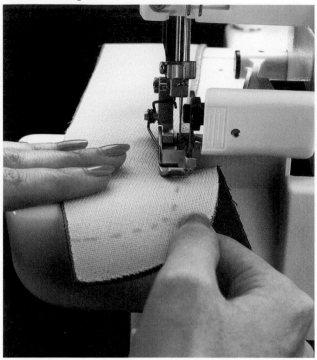

Enclosed seam. 1) Mark seamline on wrong side of collar for accurate stitching. Adjust serger for narrow balanced 3-thread stitch (pages 69 to 71). Adjust looper tensions so stitches hug edge of curve. Stitch collar pieces, right sides together, with needle on seamline.

2) Turn collar right side out. Press edge, using tip of iron to prevent seam imprint. Serged stitches flex to ease in fullness along curved edges, so clipping is unnecessary.

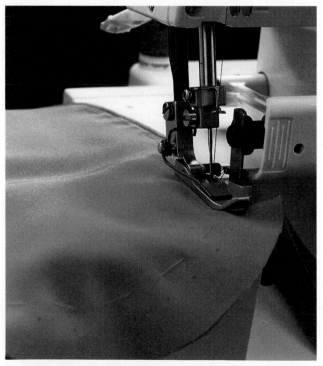

Exposed seam. Mark seamline on *right* side of collar for accurate stitching. Adjust serger for 3-thread rolled hem stitch (pages 79 to 81). Baste collar pieces, *wrong* sides together; serge, trimming away entire seam allowance.

Exposed seam with piping effect. Use topstitching thread or buttonhole twist in upper looper, and use regular thread in needle and lower looper. Mark seamline and serge, as for exposed seam, left.

How to Apply a Convertible Collar

  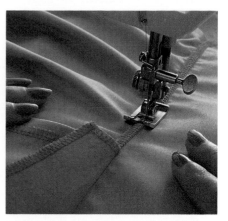

1) Stitch collar pieces, right sides together, using conventional machine. Grade seam allowances and collar points; clip. Turn collar right side out; press. Staystitch neck edge; clip to staystitching.

2) Pin collar to garment at neckline, right sides together, matching center back, shoulder seams, and center fronts. Fold front facings back on foldlines over ends of collar. Baste neckline. Remove pins.

3) Serge neckline seam, securing the tail chains (pages 38 and 39). If desired, understitch back of neckline through all layers, using conventional machine.

How to Apply a Flat or Stand-up Collar

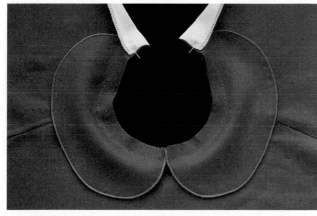 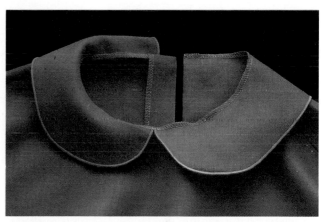

Flat collar. 1) Prepare collar, using serger or conventional method. Pin collar to garment at neckline, right sides up, matching markings; baste. Fold facings over ends of collar, right sides together.

2) Serge neckline seam, securing tail chains (pages 38 and 39). Turn facings to inside of garment; press.

 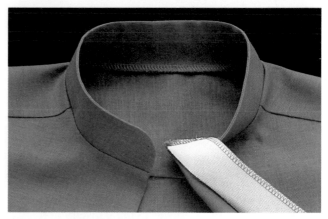

3) Lift collar; understitch on conventional machine, from right side, close to seamline, stitching through garment and seam allowances.

Stand-up collar. Follow steps 1 and 2 for flat collar, above. Press collar up.

How to Sew a Cuff without a Placket

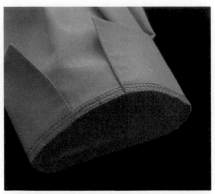

1) Stitch cuff, right sides together, using conventional machine; grade and clip seam allowances. Turn and press.

2) Prepare lower edge of sleeve, including gathers or tucks; mark, but do not slash, opening. Pin cuff to sleeve, placing ends 5/8" (1.5 cm) from slash mark. Serge seam.

3) Fold cuff down. Press seam toward sleeve. Hand-stitch or topstitch opening between ends of cuff.

How to Sew a Cuff with a Placket

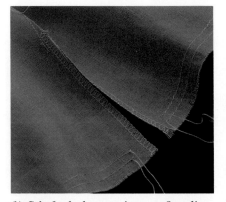

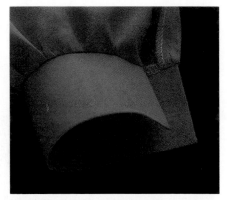

1) Stitch slash opening, as for slit (page 41). Fold, with right sides together and edges even. Using conventional machine, stitch 1" (2.5 cm) dart at end of slit. Stitch sleeve seam, and prepare lower edge of sleeve, including gathers or tucks.

2) Stitch cuff, using conventional machine; grade and clip seam allowances. Turn and press. Pin cuff to sleeve, right sides together; fold edges of slit opening over ends of cuff. Serge seam, securing tail chains (pages 36 and 37).

3) Fold cuff down. Fold and press edges of slit to inside. Press seam toward sleeve. For crisp edge, fuse 1/4" (6 mm) strip of fusible web under folds of slit.

Cuff with underlap extension. 1) Prepare slit opening, as in step 1, above. Using conventional machine, stitch ends and underlap of cuff; pivot at dot, and stitch to raw edge. Grade and clip seam allowances. Turn and press.

2) Stitch sleeve seam, and prepare lower edge of sleeve, including gathers or tucks. Pin cuff to sleeve, right sides together, folding back underlap and folding edges of slit opening over ends of cuff. Serge seam. Finish cuff, as in step 3, above.

How to Sew a Blouse Using a Serger

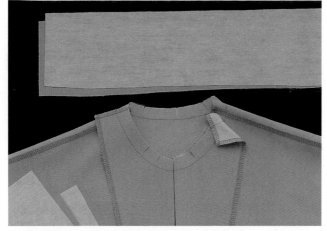

1) Apply interfacing. Staystitch and clip neckline. Finish facings. Stitch shoulder seams. If garment has raglan sleeves, stitch the sleeve seams. Press.

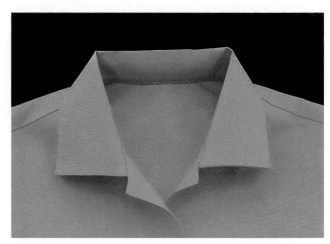

2) Prepare and apply collar, as on pages 93 to 95.

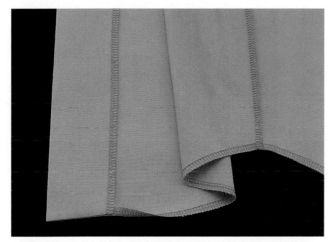

3) Stitch side seams. Fold facings to wrong side on foldlines. Serge lower edge of blouse, stitching through facings. Turn facings right side out.

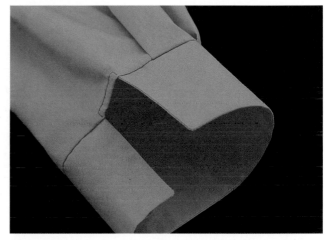

4) Stitch plackets and apply cuffs to blouse, as on pages 93 and 96.

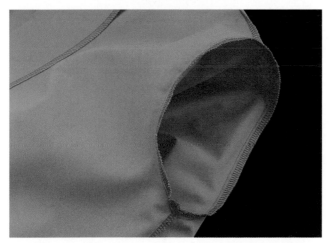

5) Set in sleeves using conventional machine, if garment has standard set-in sleeves. To finish seams, serge armhole seam, through both layers, 1/8" (3 mm) away from conventional stitching; press.

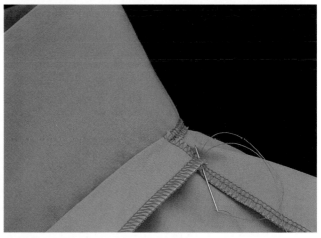

6) Turn up hem and topstitch in place (page 63). Tack front facings at shoulder seams of blouse as shown. Make buttonholes; sew on buttons. Press garment.

Skirts & Pants

The skirt or pants style and the fabric weight will help you decide which sewing techniques to use in construction. You may be able to sew the garment completely on the serger, or you may need to use both the serger and the conventional machine.

Full skirts that are made from lightweight fabrics can be sewn almost entirely on the serger. The seams are rarely subjected to a lot of stress, so an overlock seam alone is sufficient. Fitted skirts, or those made from heavier fabrics, require a 5-thread safety stitch, a mock safety stitch, or conventional seams with overedged finishes. Special seams shown on pages 49 to 52 may also be considered.

Tailored pants and skirts that have seams with a zipper opening, vent, or kick pleat, or those that may need to be altered after a fitting, require the use of a conventional machine. Also, heavier fabrics follow body curves better when conventional seams are sewn; you may want to finish the seam allowances first, using the serger, while the garment sections are still flat.

In-seam pockets on full skirts, or on skirts or pants made from knits, may be attached using the serger. The conventional method, as directed in the pattern instruction sheet, should be used to attach pockets on tailored skirts and pants.

Zipper applications require the full seam allowance and are inserted using a conventional machine. Darts are sewn on a conventional machine for accuracy, and to prevent dimples or puckers at the point. Serging darts eliminates any chance of changing the dart position at a later time.

Waistbands

There are several methods for applying waistbands. Elasticized waistbands are for pull-on skirts and pants. The edge-finished waistband is for smooth, fitted skirts and pants with waistline openings. Waistbands use both the serger and the conventional machine.

A cut-on elasticized waistband is a quick waistline finish for straight-cut skirts or pants. The upper edge of the garment is folded down to form a casing for the elastic; the elastic may be inserted or attached. The separate elasticized waistband may be cut from self-fabric; or use a lighter-weight fabric, such as ribbing, to eliminate bulk.

The elastic should pull easily over the hips and fit comfortably around the waist. Most elastics are cut 2" to 3" (5 to 7.5 cm) less than your waist measurement; soft, lightweight elastics may be cut even shorter, while very firm ones should be cut equal to your waist measurement. Multiple rows of topstitching may reduce the elastic recovery; to ensure a snug fit, the elastic is cut 1" (2.5 cm) shorter than the guidelines.

The inside edge of an edge-finished waistband is serged to reduce bulk. It encloses seams that are conventionally sewn and graded. Flatlocked or topstitched belt loops may be attached at the waistline before applying the waistband.

How to Sew Side Seams with Pockets

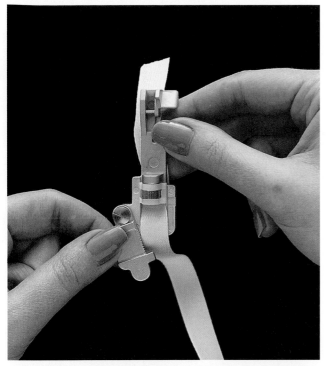

1) Cut ½" (1.3 cm) twill tape or ⅝" (1.5 cm) strip of fusible knit interfacing 1" (2.5 cm) longer than pocket opening. Slip tape through elastic tape foot, if using; loosen adjustment knob to prevent drag on tape. Attach foot to serger, holding tape behind foot.

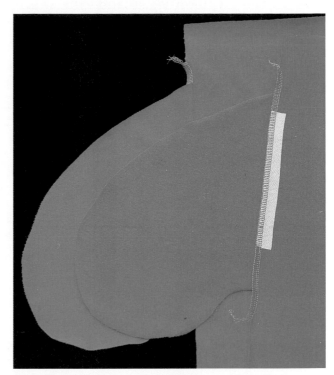

2) Apply twill tape or interfacing to seam allowance of garment; center length along front pocket opening. Serge front pocket to garment front, and back pocket to garment back. Press seams toward pockets.

3) Use conventional machine to stitch garment side seam, right sides together; stitch from about 3" (7.5 cm) below pocket opening to bottom of pocket opening. Stitch from top of pocket opening to upper edge of garment section.

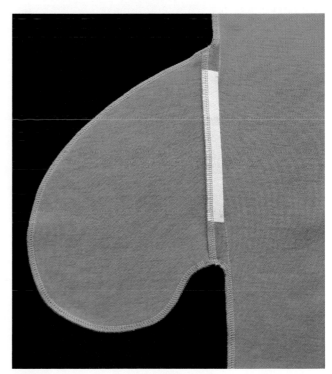

4) Sew garment side seam from lower edge to straight stitching at bottom of pocket opening; then curve stitching around pocket. Continue stitching side seam to waistline. Press pocket and side seam toward front of garment.

How to Sew a Cut-on Waistband with Attached Elastic

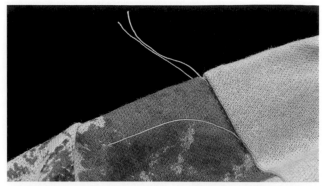

1) Extend pattern above waistline two times the width of the elastic. Cut elastic using guidelines on page 98. Lap elastic ends ½" (1.3 cm); stitch, using zigzag. Pin-mark elastic and garment edge into fourths. Pin elastic to wrong side of garment, matching pins; align edges. Serge, stretching elastic so garment lies flat; disengage knives, if desired, to avoid cutting elastic. Remove pins as you come to them.

2) Fold elastic to wrong side of garment so fabric encases elastic. Stitch in the ditch, across the elastic width, at center front, center back, and side seams; stitch from right side of garment, using conventional machine.

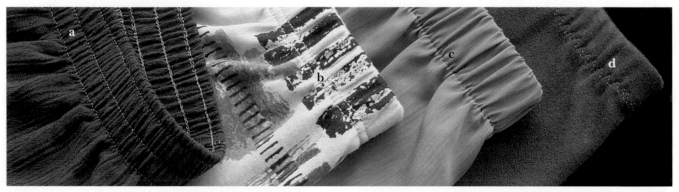

3) Topstitch through all layers of waistband, stretching elastic as you sew. Chainstitch three or more evenly spaced rows across width of elastic, using serger with disengaged knives, for low-stretch knits and wovens (**a**); cover-stitch over lower edge of casing, using serger, for maximum stretch (**b**); straight-stitch near lower edge of casing, using long stitches on a conventional machine, for wovens (**c**); or zigzag close to lower edge of casing, using conventional machine, for knits (**d**).

How to Sew a Cut-on Waistband with Elastic Insert

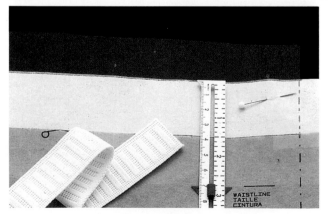

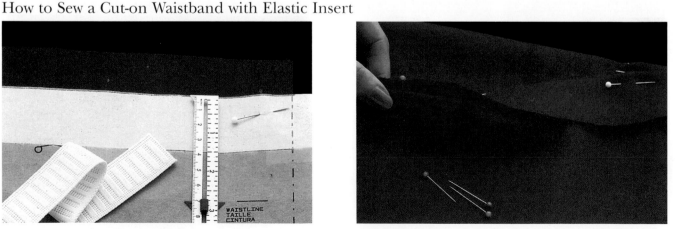

1) Extend pattern above waistline two times the width of the elastic plus ¾" (2 cm). For example, for a 1" (2.5 cm) elastic, add 2¾" (7 cm) above the waistline.

2) Fold garment to wrong side an amount equal to the width of the elastic plus ½" (1.3 cm); pin or baste. Fold garment back on itself, with raw edge extending ¼" (6 mm) beyond fold.

How to Apply a Separate Elasticized Waistband

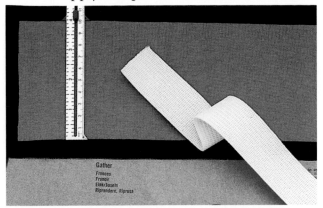

1) Cut waistband two times the width of elastic plus 1½" (3.8 cm) to allow for two ⅝" (1.5 cm) seam allowances plus ¼" (6 mm) ease. If using woven fabric, length of waistband is the same measurement as edge of garment. If using ribbing, length must be long enough to pull over hips.

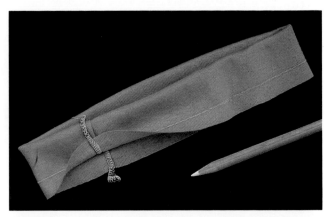

2) Mark seamlines for accurate stitching; this is especially helpful when ribbing is used. Stitch short ends of waistband, right sides together, to form a circle. Fold in half lengthwise, wrong sides together.

3) Pin band to waistline edge as on page 91, step 2; place band seam at side or center back. Overlock with needle on seamline; leave 2" (5 cm) opening for elastic insertion. If using ribbing, stretch ribbing to match garment; use differential feed (page 46), if desired.

4) Cut elastic to fit waistline, using guidelines on page 98. Lap elastic ends ½" (1.3 cm); stitch, using zigzag. Overlock opening closed. Stitch in the ditch at seamlines to prevent elastic from twisting, if desired.

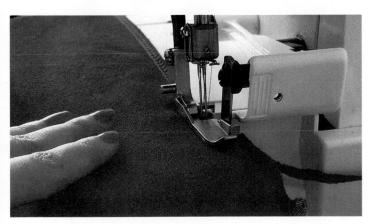

3) Stitch along the fold so stitches catch, but do not cut fold; trim extended seam allowance. Remove pins as you come to them. Leave 2" (5 cm) opening for inserting elastic.

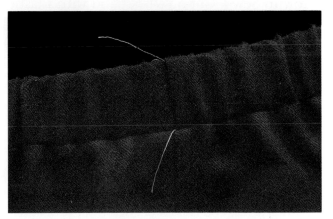

4) Cut elastic to fit waistline; insert into waistband. Lap elastic ends ½" (1.3 cm); stitch, using zigzag. Overlock opening closed. Stitch in the ditch at seamlines to prevent elastic from twisting, if desired.

How to Apply an Edge-finished Waistband

1) **Interface** waistband. Serge one long side of waistband, trimming ⅜" (1 cm).

2) **Baste** one end of each belt loop to garment at desired position. Pin waistband to garment, matching pattern markings; straight-stitch, keeping serged edge of waistband free. Grade seam allowance.

3) **Press** seam allowances toward waistband. Fold waistband, right sides together. Stitch overlap end of waistband, folding serged seam allowance back to waistline seam; grade.

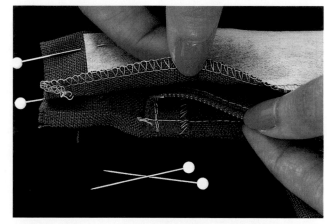

4) **Tuck** garment into the waistband at underlap end of garment.

5) **Stitch** across end and lower edge of underlap; continue stitching over previous stitches through all layers of garment and waistband; stop stitching (arrow) ½" (1.3 cm) beyond underlap dot. Grade.

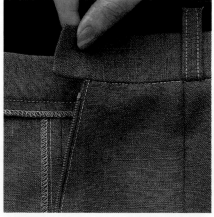

6) **Turn** waistband right side out, and press; serged edge extends down on inside of garment. Pin in place. Stitch in the ditch of the seam from right side, using conventional sewing machine.

7) **Fold** under free end of each belt loop; topstitch to waistband at upper edge.

How to Sew Belt Loops

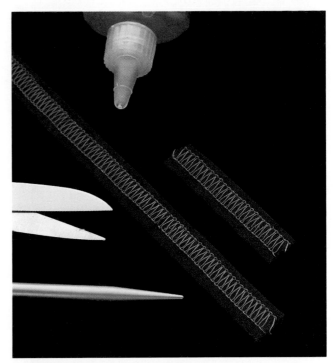

Flatlock belt loops. 1) Cut fabric strip two times the finished width of belt loop; length of strip equals cut length of each belt loop times the number of loops. Fold strip lengthwise, wrong sides together; do not press. Serge long edges together, using flatlock stitch (pages 74 to 77).

2) Insert pencil or knitting needle inside tube to flatten stitches. Center stitches on underside of strip; press. Mark cutting lines. Apply liquid fray preventer at marks; allow to dry. Cut into belt loops.

Topstitched belt loops. 1) Cut strip of fabric three times the finished width of belt loop; length of strip equals cut length of each belt loop times number of loops. Serge one long edge of strip, trimming slightly.

2) Fold strip into thirds lengthwise, enclosing raw edge. Topstitch both edges from right side ⅛" (3 mm) from fold. Mark cutting lines. Apply liquid fray preventer at marks; allow to dry. Cut into belt loops.

Dresses

The techniques used for serging blouses and skirts (pages 93 to 103) are also used for the bodice and skirt sections of dresses. The sections are joined using one of several waistline methods.

Dresses with gathered skirts may be serged using either method on page 51. Dresses with pleated skirts use conventional construction methods for the waistline seam; the seam allowances are serged for a neat, durable finish.

When the serger is used to add elastic to dresses without waistline seams, it reduces the bulk of the usual bias tape casing. Narrow transparent elastic or ⅛" (3 mm) oval elastic can be secured using a flatlock stitch. This method may also be used on gathered cuffs or puffed sleeves, especially popular in children's wear and sleepwear.

Two methods are available for serging elasticized waistline seams on dresses. Elastic may be inserted into a casing formed by serging the seam allowances together as shown, opposite. Or, the elastic may be serged to the skirt before sewing the waistline seam.

An elastic tape foot can be used to make narrow elastic applications easier; since methods vary between models, refer to your instruction manual. The instructions for applying elastic on the opposite page do not require special accessories and can be done on any serger.

Belt loops may be added after the waistline seam is finished. Chain belt loops have the look of hand-crocheted loops and can be made quickly using tail chains. Sturdier chain loops can be serged over buttonhole twist, pearl cotton, or topstitching thread, using the rolled hem; the special gimp presser foot helps make these belt loops easy.

How to Overedge Elastic at a Placement Line

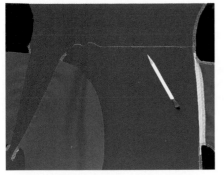

1) Mark elastic placement line on wrong side of garment pieces. Stitch and press seams, leaving a side seam open. Fold garment on placement line. Adjust machine for flatlock stitch (pages 74 to 77).

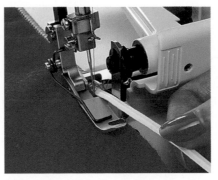

2) Position ⅛" (3 mm) elastic under back of presser foot, bringing elastic over foot at front. Stitch along placement line, with elastic between needle and knife; do not stretch elastic or cut fold.

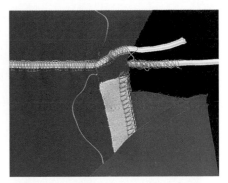

3) Pull fabric to flatten fold. Pull elastic to fit. Secure elastic ends using conventional machine. Stitch remaining side seam; trim excess elastic. (Ladder of flatlock stitches shows on right side of garment.)

How to Insert Elastic in a Waistline Seam Casing

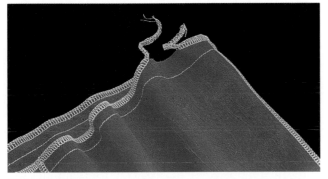

1) Stitch waistline seam, using conventional machine. Serge seam allowances together, trimming slightly; leave 2" (5 cm) opening for inserting elastic.

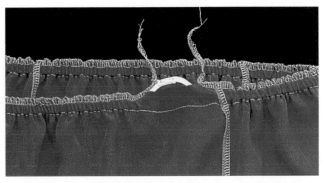

2) Cut elastic, using guidelines on page 98; insert into casing. Stitch lapped ends of elastic together, using conventional machine. Serge opening closed. Turn casing toward bodice; topstitch near serged edge.

How to Apply Elastic to a Waistline Seam

Cut elastic (page 98). Lap ends ½" (1.3 cm); zigzag. Quarter elastic and skirt, using pins. Pin elastic to right side of skirt, just above seamline, matching pins. Serge elastic, trimming seam allowance only; stretch elastic so skirt lies flat. Trim bodice seam allowance to elastic width. Stitch skirt to bodice, right sides together, using zipper foot. Turn seam allowance up; topstitch, stretching elastic, to enclose raw edge.

How to Attach a Chain Belt Loop

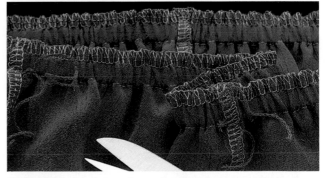

Cut tail chain three times the finished loop length. Stitch chain through garment, using hand needle, so ends are on inside. Adjust loop length on right side of garment. Tie ends of chain together; clip excess.

Sewing Special Fabrics

Many fabrics require special handling for best results. The weave, pattern, design, and weight of the fabric all affect the finished seams. To anticipate problems, always test-sew on fabric scraps across both grainlines and on the bias before constructing a garment.

Many sergers have a differential feed system (page 46), which can be used on special fabrics. This feature is helpful when sewing lightweight fabrics that pucker, such as sheers, or fabrics that stretch out of shape easily, such as sweater knits and bias-cut fabrics.

Sheers (1) and **silkies (2)** require a new needle (size 70/10 or 75/11) and a shorter stitch length (1.5 to 2 mm). Use taut sewing, below, or differential feed when stitching these lightweight fabrics to prevent puckered seams. If necessary, the needle thread tension may also be loosened slightly to prevent puckering, but this may cause needle thread to show on the right side of the garment.

Laces (3) require a short stitch length (2 mm) and a narrow stitch width (2.5 to 3.5 mm). Use taut sewing or differential feed to prevent puckering. Uneven stitching cannot be avoided because of thick and thin areas on lace. Open-weave laces may not have enough surface on which the serger can stitch. A strip of tricot bias binding can be sewn into the seam to give a complete surface for the serger to stitch.

Fabrics with raised designs (4), such as matelassé and eyelet, may also cause irregular stitches due to their uneven textures. For this reason, do not use decorative stitching on these fabrics. Plan for seamlines to fall between eyelet embroideries, if possible; and if using a rolled hem finish on eyelet, plan for the stitches to fall between individual eyelet designs.

Preventing Puckered or Stretched Seams

Adjusting differential feed. Adjust the differential feed feature, if available on your serger, to prevent puckered or stretched seams. The setting will differ, depending on the fabric. Stitch without taut sewing or easing fabric, allowing machine to feed fabric automatically.

Taut sewing. Hold fabric firmly in front of and behind the presser foot while stitching, to prevent puckered seams. Do not pull fabric through the machine. Sew at an even speed for smooth stitching.

Sweater knit fabrics (5) and some **polar fleece fabrics (6)** require special handling to prevent stretched seams. Use the differential feed if your serger has this feature, or ease the fabric into the machine, below. For more information on sewing sweater knits, see pages 108 and 109.

Bulky fabrics (7) such as boiled wools and quilted fabrics may be too thick to feed into the knives, restricting the trimming function of the machine. Compress the thick layers with a row of straight or zigzag stitches, using a conventional machine. Sew, allowing the knives to cut on this stitching line.

Decorator fabrics (8) can be serged easily. For easier stitching of large pieces, such as drapery panels, do not allow the fabric to hang over the edge of the table. Trim away selvages as you stitch drapery seams, to avoid puckering.

Fake fur (9) can be seamed with the flatlock stitch (pages 74 to 77) to eliminate bulky and twisted seams. Completely trim away the seam allowances before sewing, and place the fur right sides together, pushing fur fibers away from the seamline. Then flatlock the seam without trimming, and pull the seam flat.

Coated fabrics (10), such as rain-resistant outerwear, may feed unevenly through the feed system. Adjust the differential feed as necessary, or control the fabric layers manually as shown below.

Easing fabric. Hold fabric loosely in front of the presser foot, allowing the machine to feed it readily, to prevent stretched seams. Do not hold fabric behind the presser foot.

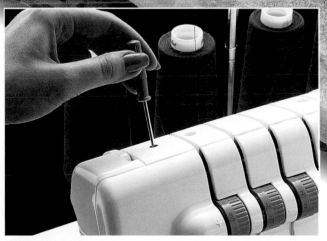

Adjusting presser foot pressure. Factory-set pressure is good for most fabrics. Turn pressure-regulating control clockwise to increase pressure on lightweight fabrics; turn it counterclockwise to decrease pressure on heavyweight fabrics. Increase pressure to stretch the top layer slightly if differential feed is not available.

Sweaters

Sweater fabrics are available in several forms. Sweater bodies, panels with prefinished ribbed edges, are available with ribbing to match. Sweater knit yardage can be purchased on the bolt with ribbing yardage to match; or knit your own sweater yardage or panels using a knitting machine or by hand.

Cut sweater knit fabric allowing 1" (2.5 cm) seam allowances, except for ribbing seams. The serger handles the fabric better, without stretching it, when a larger seam allowance is trimmed. Cut and fit ribbing for necklines or cuffs, as directed below, allowing ¼" (6 mm) seam allowances.

Sweater knit fabric may stretch out of shape when sewn. To prevent seams from stretching, use the differential feed if your machine has this feature, or ease the fabric under the presser foot as you stitch (pages 106 and 107). To sew sweater knits, 3-thread overlock or 4/3-thread mock safety stitches may be used, but they may not recover well when stretched. You may prefer the 4-thread or 5-thread safety stitches, which are more stable.

How to Cut a Sweater Body

1) Lay sweater body on cutting surface that can be pinned into. Stretch ribbed edge to same size as body of panel; pin to cutting surface.

2) Fold up hem allowance on pattern, if included. Lay pattern on fabric with fold at ribbed edge. Cut, allowing 1" (2.5 cm) seam allowances.

3) Cut neckline ribbing, using the pattern guide. Check fit of ribbing around neck, opposite.

How to Cut Ribbing

Straight edges. Fold ribbing in half lengthwise; pin-fit around body. Ribbing should lie flat without gaping. Do not distort ribs. Add ½" (1.3 cm) for seam allowances.

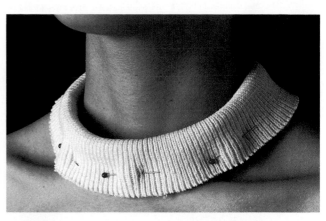

Necklines. Cut ribbing according to pattern guide. Stitch ribbing seam, and fold in half lengthwise. Check fit around neck; adjust ribbing seam, if necessary.

Tips for Sweater Knit Seams

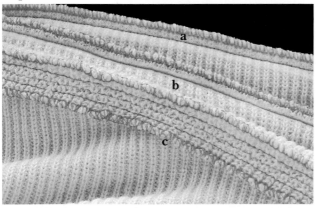

Stabilize shoulder seams with transparent elastic (**a**) or tricot bias binding (**b**), as on page 53. Or use a conventional seam with serged seam finishes, and edgestitch seam on each side (**c**).

Sew sleeves to garment; do not stretch the armhole. Place sleeve over armhole to ease sleeve with your hands; place sleeve under armhole to ease sleeve using differential feed.

How to Apply Ribbing to a Sweater

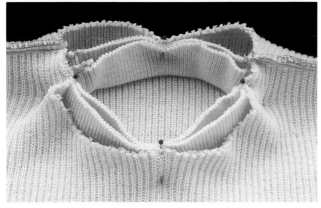

1) Stitch ends of ribbing, right sides together; fold in half lengthwise. Divide ribbing and garment edges into fourths; mark. Pin ribbing to garment, right sides together, matching markings.

2) Stitch with ribbing on top. Ease garment edge to match ribbing; do not stretch garment or ribbing.

Activewear

Sergers that have stretch stitches are perfect for sewing activewear. A 3-thread or 4-thread mock safety stitch, a cover stitch, or a 3-thread overlock stitch is recommended for strong, stretchy seams that stretch with two-way stretch fabrics, allowing for comfort and unrestricted action.

Stitches should be tested on both lengthwise and crosswise grains of fabric scraps before sewing the garment. Looper thread tension dials should be adjusted so the threads lock at the fabric edge. Needle threads should be just loose enough to prevent thread breakage when stretched, and as tight as necessary to prevent threads from showing noticeably on the right side of the fabric.

Activewear seams have a tendency to pull open and expose the needle threads, even when tensions are adjusted, because of the close fit of the garment. Thread that closely matches the fabric makes this less noticeable. Texturized nylon thread is also helpful. When used in the needle, it tightens up the stitches yet stretches with the fabric. When it is used in the loopers, seams are soft, comfortable, and strong; this is important for close-fitting garments.

The in-the-round method of construction is recommended for smooth, strong elasticized edges. Elastic is easy to apply in the round because you can stretch the elastic in front of and behind the presser foot at

all times. When the flat method or elastic tape foot is used, a few extra inches (centimeters) of elastic, extending behind the presser foot, makes starting the seam easier.

For improved fit around upper leg openings, such as on swimwear, elastic is not applied evenly. Less elastic is used in the back, where a tighter fit will keep the fabric cupped under the seat. When sewing in-the-round, shift the elastic slightly toward the leg front. When using the elastic tape foot, practice changing the tension applied to the elastic; apply minimal tension at the leg front and increase the applied tension at the leg back.

Transparent elastic or chlorine-resistant elastic is used for sewing swimwear. Transparent elastic, lighter in weight than chlorine-resistant elastic, gives a smoother fit. There is also less concern about cutting into transparent elastic with the knives because it does not fray when trimmed.

Narrow decorative piping that stretches with the seam can be made using decorative threads (pages 118 and 119), wide transparent elastic, and the 3-thread rolled hem stitch. Serge wider piping using the wrapped overedge stitch (page 115). Soft decorative threads, such as rayon or texturized nylon, are recommended; swimwear piping that will be subjected to chlorine should be made using texturized nylon.

How to Apply Elastic on a Swimsuit Leg

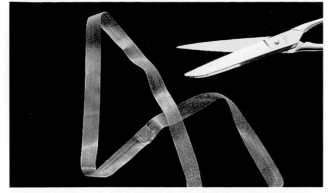

1) Cut elastic ½" to 1½" (1.3 to 3.8 cm) shorter than measurement of swimsuit leg opening. Lap ends ½" (1.3 cm); stitch on conventional machine.

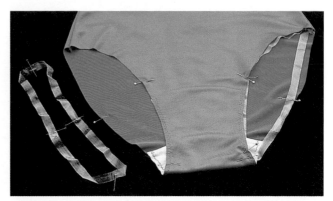

2) Quarter elastic and leg opening, using pins. Pin elastic to wrong side of swimsuit, with inside edge of elastic on seamline; match two pins at leg front and two pins at leg back. Shift two remaining elastic marks about ½" (1.3 cm) toward front of remaining suit marks; pin.

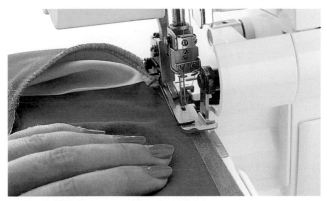

3) Stitch, using long stitches; trim seam allowance to elastic width, if necessary. Do not cut elastic with knives. Remove pins as they approach knives.

4) Fold elastic to inside of suit. Topstitch from the right side, using cover stitch. Or, on conventional machine, use long stitches, twin needle, loosened bobbin tension, and texturized nylon thread in the bobbin.

How to Make and Apply Decorative Elastic Piping

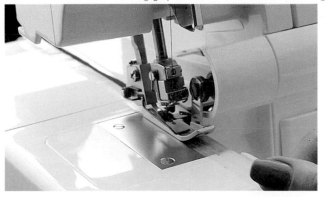

1) Adjust machine for rolled hem stitch (pages 79 to 81) or 3-thread wrapped overedge (page 115), and shorten stitch length; use decorative thread in needle and both loopers, or in upper looper as desired. Stitch along elastic edge, trimming elastic slightly; avoid stretching elastic.

2) Adjust machine for a stretch stitch; attach cording foot. Stitch onto elastic until rolled edge rests under foot groove. Position fabric, right sides together, in front of foot to sandwich piping between layers; align fabric edges so rolled edge follows seamline, and elastic lies on seam allowance.

Special Effects

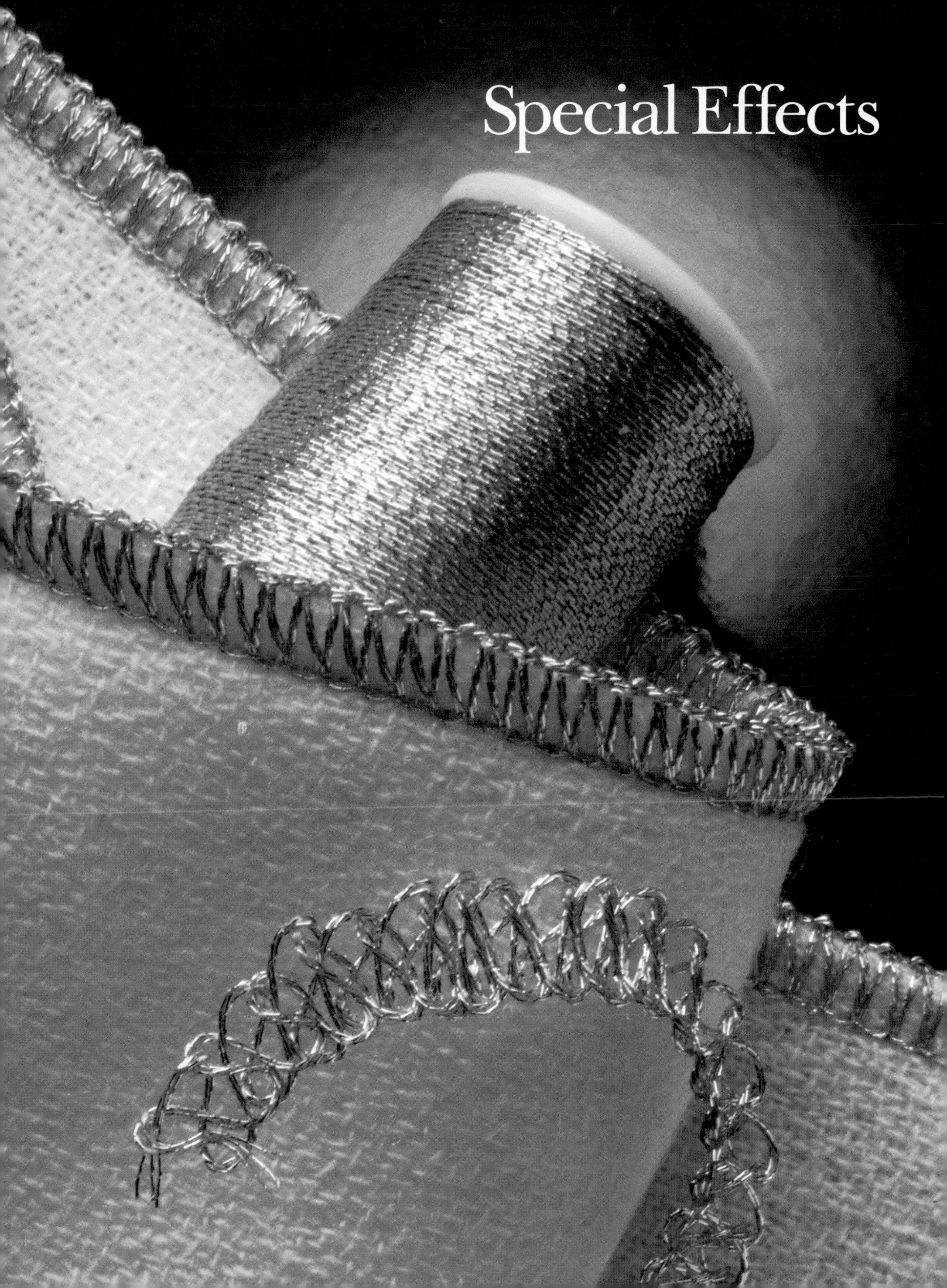

Special Decorative Stitches

The use of decorative threads on a serger or overlock can duplicate the look of fine braids and bindings previously found only in ready-to-wear. Decorative threads for use in a serger can be found in fabric, craft, needlework, and yarn stores, as well as through sewing machine dealers.

The finished effect of the decorative thread depends on the width and length of the stitch as well as on the thread being used. When using decorative techniques, it is important to test-sew each thread and fabric to determine how to achieve the desired result. Practice sewing with a variety of stitch length, width, and tension adjustments.

Interfacing or tricot bias binding may be used to stabilize decorative edge finishes on moderate-stretch knits, bias-cut fabrics, or laces. Narrow strips of fusible interfacings should be applied to the wrong side of the fabric. Strips of nonfusible interfacing or binding may be placed on top of the fabric and trimmed away as shown on page 63.

If a decorative thread is lightweight, strong, and does not fray, it can be used in the needles and loopers. When decorative thread is used only in a looper, it lies on the fabric surface because the looper threads do not penetrate the fabric. Usually, a decorative thread is only used for the looper thread that forms the most visible part of the stitch, and regular sewing thread or fine monofilament nylon thread is used in the other looper and needle.

Special effects are possible by changing the colors of threads used, opposite. The 3-thread flatlock stitch is shown; similar effects are possible in the rolled hem stitch and the 2-thread flatlock stitch.

Other special effects are possible by thread-blending. Small stands with multiple spool pins are available; they slip onto a serger's spool pin and allow the threads to feed through thread guides as one thread. You can create your own decorative thread by using more than one color of regular thread in a looper. You can strengthen a fragile decorative thread by blending it with monofilament nylon, and blending two matching threads gives fine threads more impact.

It is often easier to use decorative thread in the upper looper than in the lower looper. There are fewer thread guides for the upper looper thread to follow, and decorative threads are less likely to fray or break. For this reason, if you have a choice between using a 2-thread or a 3-thread flatlock on your serger, you may prefer 3-thread flatlocking when using heavier decorative threads.

Reversed Stitches

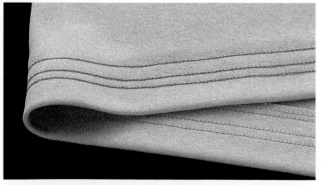

Chainstitch. Disengage knives. Use decorative thread in looper, and change stitch length, if desired. Adjust thread tension dials, if necessary. Serge linear or gently curving pattern, wrong side up. Use tear-away or water-soluble stabilizer, if stitching on single layer of lightweight to mediumweight fabric.

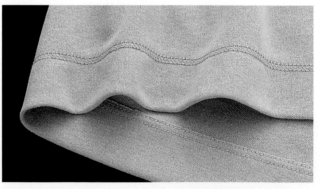

Cover Stitch. Disengage knives. Use decorative thread in the looper, if desired. Serge, wrong side up. Use water-soluble stabilizer, which can be removed without distorting the looper thread formation, if stitching on a single fabric layer.

The Effects of Thread Placement in a 3-Thread Flatlock

Monochromatic. Use decorative thread in the upper looper and matching regular sewing thread in the needle and lower looper.

Enclosed or outlined. Use decorative thread in the upper looper and a contrasting color in both the needle and lower looper.

Free or floating. Use decorative thread in the upper looper and monofilament thread in both the needle and lower looper.

Reversible Stitches

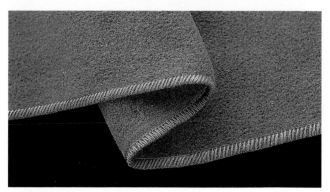

3-thread Wrapped Overedge Stitches. Use decorative thread in the upper looper. Loosen upper looper thread tension dial so thread wraps completely around the edge; tighten lower looper thread tension dial until lower looper thread forms a straight line.

2-thread Wrapped Overedge Stitches. Use decorative thread in the lower looper. Loosen looper thread tension dial so thread wraps completely around the edge; tighten needle thread tension dial to hold stitches taut. (Upper and chainstitch loopers are not threaded when using a 5-thread serger.)

Adjusting the Decorative Stitch

The stitch width and stitch length control not only how wide or how far apart the stitches will be, but also the final appearance of the decorative stitching.

For stitch length, the general rule of adjustment is: the finer the thread, the shorter the stitch length. Short stitches (1 to 2 mm) are used for fine, lightweight threads to make the stitching more noticeable. Heavier threads require a longer stitch length (4 to 5 mm) to allow for the thickness of the thread, so it can lie in even curves on the fabric. Heavy threads do not curve and bend as easily with short stitches. When stitches are too close together, the loops of heavy thread may pile up, causing a fabric jam.

Varying the stitch width also changes the appearance of the stitching. Stitch width is mostly a matter of personal preference, but, generally, a narrower stitch is used with fine, lightweight threads; a wider stitch, with heavy threads.

How to Test-sew Decorative Thread

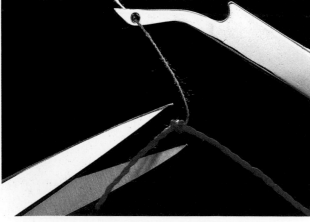

1) Thread serger, tying on threads (pages 30 and 31); do not pull the knots through loopers when using heavy thread.

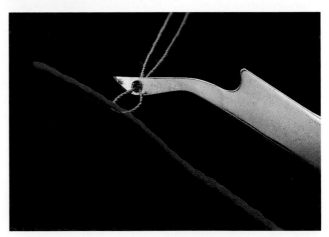

2) Use strand of all-purpose thread to form a loop; thread through eye of looper. Place the decorative thread through the loop, and pull through the eye.

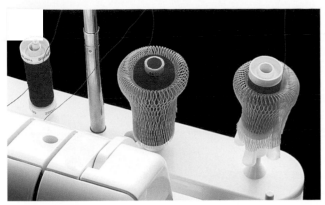

3) Use a net on thread if thread tends to slide or spill off the spool or for any thread that feeds unevenly. Turn top of net down to prevent net from causing uneven feeding.

4) Test-sew slowly without fabric. Watch the area around stitch fingers to see if stitches are forming.

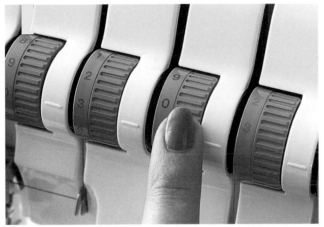

5) Loosen tension if thread does not feed through serger. It may be necessary to loosen tension completely or skip a thread guide if it pinches the thread. (On some sergers, you may need to bypass tension disc.)

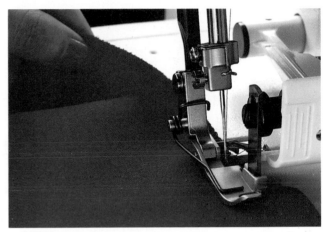

6) Lift presser foot, and place fabric scrap under foot; stitch slowly, checking stitch formation on fabric. Adjust tension, stitch length, and stitch width, until desired stitch is achieved.

Tips for Serging with Decorative Thread

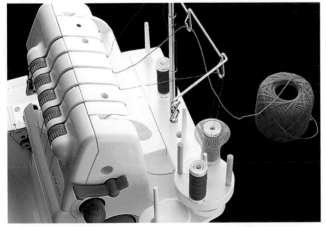

Feed ball, skein, and card threads directly into first thread guide. Reel thread off by hand. Keep decorative thread slack near thread guide holder; it is important to watch for this while serging to prevent uneven stitches. Slip a multiple spool stand on a serger spool pin to blend threads.

Place cardboard shim under presser foot before and after an intersecting seam, so stitch length remains even at thick seam allowances; position shim so needle does not stitch through it.

Selecting Decorative Threads

Not all decorative threads will work in all sergers. Test threads (pages 116 to 117) to find out which will be most successful for you. Do not assume that, because a certain thread works in your friend's machine, it will also work in yours. If your machine does not handle a certain thread well, you may be able to find a substitute that gives a similar effect.

When experimenting with decorative threads in the serger, start with lightweight and smooth-textured threads, which require fewer tension adjustments. Avoid quilting thread; although it is lightweight, it is too stiff to feed easily through the machine. Check your instruction manual to see if you can use the special embroidery needles with longer eyes.

The amount of decorative thread required varies, depending on the size of the thread, the stitch length and width, and the total length of decorative stitching. Each looper, or needle with loosened tension, usually requires 9 to 10 yards (8.25 to 9.15 m) of decorative thread per yard (0.95 m) of decorative stitching; a lightweight thread will require more yardage for complete coverage. To estimate how much thread you will need for each looper or needle, multiply the distance to be sewn with decorative stitches, plus 1 yard (0.95 m) for test-sewing, by at least nine.

Monofilament nylon, topstitching thread, and texturized nylon are the easiest decorative threads to use in a serger. They require minor tension adjustments and can be used in both loopers, and in the needles.

Fine monofilament nylon (1) can be used to blend stitches with the fabric, such as for rolled hems on multicolored fabrics. Or use it in the needle and lower looper when sewing a 3-thread overlock stitch, with a heavy decorative thread in the upper looper; the nylon thread blends into the decorative loops.

Topstitching thread (2) or buttonhole twist can be used in loopers and needles, but is most often used in loopers only, with regular or monofilament thread in the needles. Use topstitching thread or buttonhole twist in the upper and lower looper to sew a balanced 3-thread overlock stitch that is decorative, although not identical, on both sides of the fabric.

Texturized nylon thread (3) is easy to use on the serger, although it has a fuzzy appearance. It is soft, comfortable, and strong, and is ideal for activewear and swimwear. Texturized nylon adds tension, making it perfect for use in the lower looper when sewing a 3-thread rolled hem or 3-thread flatlock stitch. Tension can be loosened on texturized nylon thread for a lofty, filled-in edge finish. It is available in regular and heavy weight.

Rayon, silk, and metallic threads require more tension adjustment, but are not difficult to use. They are easier to use in the upper looper than in the lower looper.

Rayon (4) and **silk (5)** threads are available in several weights. Because the threads are very smooth, use nets to prevent them from spilling off the spool and to control them with a little extra tension on the

spool. Also, tighten the tension dial to prevent them from slipping between the tension discs.

Metallic thread (6) is available in gold, silver, and colors. Some metallics will fray if used in the lower looper. There are several different types of metallic thread, some more fragile than others. For easier serging, select filament threads, which do not fray or strip easily from the core.

Crochet thread, pearl cotton, ribbon, and yarn are the heaviest or thickest decorative threads and require a greater amount of tension adjustment. They may not feed well through the lower looper. It may be necessary to loosen the tension dial as much as possible. To ensure even feeding of balls or skeins, feed the thread by hand, making sure there is always slack in the thread as it enters the first thread guide (page 117).

Crochet thread (7) is available in cotton or acrylic and comes wound in balls. It is tightly twisted and can be used in both loopers.

Pearl cotton (8) also comes wound in balls and is available in two weights, #8 and #5. The #8 thread is finer and easier to use. Pearl cotton is less twisted than crochet cotton. It works well in the upper looper, but may fray if used in the lower looper.

Ribbon (9) up to ¼" (6 mm) wide can be used if it is lightweight, soft, and pliable, such as ribbons designed for knitting. You may find knitting ribbon

on cones, spools, or cards. It is available in acrylic, cotton, rayon, and silk. Polyester ribbon is usually not pliable enough to be used in the looper, but can be laid flat and overedged with a serged stitch (page 120) for a decorative effect.

Yarn (10) must be smooth and tightly twisted to feed evenly through the machine. It also must be fine enough to thread through the eye of the upper looper easily and strong enough to feed through the thread guides. Yarn tends to stretch as it is sewn, so you may need to loosen the tension completely.

Tips for Selecting Decorative Threads

Select thread with a smooth, tight twist. Thread that is spun unevenly or that has a nubby texture does not feed smoothly.

Select thread that is strong. Thread that frays or has weak, thin areas will break easily.

Select soft, flexible threads that slide smoothly through the thread guides and the eye of the looper. Thread that is stiff or nonpliable does not feed smoothly.

Select thread that can be threaded through the eye of the looper without resistance. Thread that is too heavy or thick can break the looper or disturb the timing of the machine.

Select thread of an appropriate weight for the fabric. Thread that is too heavy causes puckering.

Select thread that has the same care method as the fabric.

119

Ideas for Decorative Stitches

Use fine wool thread or yarn to overedge single layers of felted wool (**a**); a 4-thread mock safety stitch is shown. The cover stitch adds a tailored topstitching effect at seamlines (**b**).

Create smocking (**a**) by stitching parallel rows of chainstitch; use a tear-away stabilizer and elastic thread in the looper. Use tricot bias binding for soft decorative piping (**b**) (page 111). Apply lace and ribbons to hems (**c**) and folded edges (**d**), following directions at right. Use the cover stitch to secure 1/4" (6 mm) ribbons quickly (**e**).

How to Apply Lace at Hem

Use lace foot, if available, and right needle. Place lace on fabric, right sides together, so straight edge of lace is on hemline, at least 1/8" (3 mm) from fabric edge. Overlock, trimming fabric to lace edge. Press lace down.

How to Apply Trims on Fold

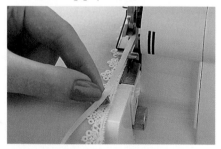

Fold fabric, wrong sides together, on placement line; press. Align trim edges on fold. Use lace foot, if available. Or use regular presser foot, above; place lace on fabric, right side up, and hold ribbon over front of presser foot between knife and needle. Serge; avoid cutting fold or trims. Extend upper trim over fold, and use flatlock, if opened fold is desired.

Finish evening bag edges with decorative threads (**a**). Use spaghetti straps (below) for a looped closure (**b**) and braided handle (**c**). Wrap a bundle of blended-thread rolled hem tail chains for a tassel (**d**). Serge a wide 3-thread tail chain of decorative threads for embellishment (**e**); couch it on, using a conventional machine. Apply beads (below) to decorate a hair bow (**f**).

How to Make Spaghetti Straps

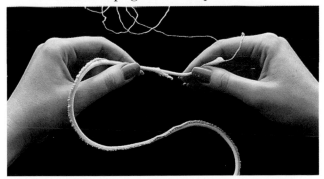

Serge tail chain 6" (15 cm) longer than desired strap length; use 2-thread chain for lightweight fabrics. Center chain on right side of fabric strip. Fold fabric over chain; use rolled hem stitch to sew raw edges together. Pull excess chain length to pull strap right side out. Use bias fabric strip for flexible straps.

How to Apply Beading

Set machine as desired: a rolled hem stitch lays beads on the edge, for a reversible finish (shown); a 3-thread overlock lays beads at the edge; and flat-locking on a fold couches beads across the fabric. Use monofilament nylon thread in right needle and loopers. Remove presser foot; use beading foot, if available. Adjust length to match bead size; move threads around beads, if necessary.

Decorative Ideas for the Home

Sergers are great timesavers when you are sewing for the home. Trim selvages from long drapery seams as you stitch, or neatly finish gathered seams and hems on swags or ruffled curtains. Add finishing touches to a project with decorative stitches and threads.

Christmas Stockings. Trim a cuff with decorative top-stitching (**a**) (page 114). Serge custom piping (**b**) and a hanger (**c**), using a cording foot. Float ribbon floss on the cuff edge (**d**), and add a blended-thread tassel (**e**) (page 114). Use decorative thread in lower looper and monofilament nylon in upper looper to create fagoting with the flatlock (**f**). Serge passementerie braid, following directions at right, and couch it on fabric using the conventional machine (**g**).

How to Make Passementerie Braid

Set differential feed (page 46) to ease. Use decorative thread in upper looper. Roll-hem the edge of wide tricot bias binding, trimming slightly; avoid stretching binding. Change to left needle and 3-thread overlock; use cording foot, if available. Change decorative thread, if desired. Serge other side of binding, aligning needle next to rolled hem.

Use two colors of thread for a special effect on project edges. Use a balanced 2-thread overedge stitch (page 73), or a balanced 3-thread overlock stitch (shown, pages 69 to 71) with decorative threads in the loopers.

Guest towels. Use short stitches and rayon thread for satin-edged fringed hems (**a**). Serge rows of pintucks (**b**), following directions below. Add rows of ladder stitches (**c**) by flatlocking on a fold (page 52) with fabric folded *right* sides together; weave a silk ribbon under some stitches, using a hand needle.

How to Sew a Pintuck

Fold fabric, wrong sides together, on placement line; press. Disengage upper knife. Serge, using balanced 3-thread overlock stitch (pages 69 to 71); align fabric fold to edge of needle plate. Press pintuck to one side.

Troubleshooting Chart

Problem	Possible Solutions	Page Reference
Fabric puckers	**Check** threading.	pages 30 and 31
	Check for tangled or caught thread.	pages 30 and 31
	Use high-quality lightweight thread.	page 22
	Shorten stitch length.	pages 66 and 67
	Loosen thread tension.	pages 69 to 83
	Use differential-feed feature, if available.	pages 46 and 106
	Hold fabric taut in front of and behind presser foot while sewing.	page 106
	Decrease presser foot pressure.	pages 106 and 107
	Check alignment and sharpness of knives.	page 27
Fabric stretches	**Trim** 1/4" (6 mm) or more while sewing; for sweater knits, trim 3/4" (2 cm), except when applying ribbing.	pages 106 and 108
	Lengthen stitch length.	pages 66 and 67
	Use differential-feed feature, if available.	pages 46 and 106
	Ease fabric into serger while sewing; do not stretch fabric.	page 107
	Stabilize seam.	pages 49 and 53
	Decrease presser foot pressure.	pages 106 and 107
Fabric jams	**Close** looper cover before sewing.	page 12
	Do not allow trimmings to fall into machine.	page 43
	Check for tangled or caught thread.	pages 30 and 31
	Compress thick layers of fabric with conventional stitches before serging.	pages 43 and 106
	Lengthen stitch length.	pages 66 and 67
	Loosen looper thread tensions.	pages 69 to 83
	Check alignment and sharpness of knives.	page 27
Fabric does not feed well	**Lower** presser foot.	page 56
	Lengthen stitch length.	pages 66 and 67
	Use differential-feed feature, if available.	pages 46 and 106
	Adjust presser foot pressure.	pages 106 and 107
	Check alignment and sharpness of knives.	page 27
Fabric layers shift at beginning of seam	**Lift** presser foot, and position fabric under it.	page 56
	Pin-baste fabric layers.	page 54
Fabric edge is uneven	**Trim** at least slightly while stitching.	page 33
	Shorten stitch length.	pages 66 and 67
	Use tricot bias binding to eliminate ragged edges on rolled hems.	page 63
	Use heavy decorative thread in looper to fill in stitches.	pages 118 and 119
	Check alignment and sharpness of knives.	page 27

Problem	Possible Solutions	Page Reference
Stitches skip	**Check** threading.	pages 30 and 31
	Use high-quality thread.	page 22
	Change type of thread.	page 22
	Insert needle correctly.	page 27
	Tighten needle set screw.	page 27
	Change a dull, damaged, or defective needle to a new needle.	page 27
	Change type or size of needle; confirm that both needles are the same size, if using two needles.	page 27
	Loosen thread tension.	pages 69 to 83
	Allow serger to feed fabric, or hold fabric taut in front of and behind presser foot while sewing.	page 106
	Do not pull fabric through machine from behind presser foot.	page 106
	Increase presser foot pressure.	pages 106 and 107
Stitches are irregular	**Check** threading.	pages 30 and 31
	Thread must feed from spool smoothly.	pages 30, 31, and 117
	Use high-quality, evenly twisted thread.	pages 22, 118, and 119
	Adjust thread tension.	pages 69 to 83, and 117 to 119
	Insert needle correctly.	page 27
	Change a dull, damaged, or defective needle to a new needle.	page 27
	Change type or size of needle; confirm that both needles are the same size, if using two needles.	page 27
	Use fabric that has an even texture for decorative stitching.	page 106
	Check alignment and sharpness of knives.	page 27
Stitches form off fabric edge	**Use** left needle.	page 27
	Widen seam width, using stitch width regulator.	page 12
Needle breaks	**Check** for tangled or caught thread.	pages 30 and 31
	Insert needle correctly.	page 27
	Tighten needle set screw.	page 27
	Change to larger-size needle.	page 27
	Do not pull fabric through machine from behind presser foot.	page 106
Thread breaks	**Check** threading.	pages 30 and 31
	Check for tangled or caught thread.	pages 30 and 31
	Use high-quality, strong thread.	pages 22, 118, and 119
	Loosen thread tension.	pages 69 to 83, and 117 to 119
	Insert needle correctly.	page 27
	Change a dull, damaged, or defective needle to a new needle.	page 27

Index